Stars and Planets

Stars and Planets

Ian Ridpath

Hamlyn
London · New York · Sydney · Toronto

Endpaper Omega nebula in Sagittarius.
Title spread Jupiter as it might appear from its moon, Ganymede.

Artwork by Gordon Davies

Published by The Hamlyn Publishing Group Limited
London · New York · Sydney · Toronto
Astronaut House, Feltham, Middlesex, England

Copyright © The Hamlyn Publishing Group Limited,
   1978
ISBN 0 600 38258 3

Phototypeset by Filmtype Services Limited,
   Scarborough, England
Colour separations by Vidicolour Limited, Herts,
   England
Printed in Spain by Mateu Cromo

Contents

Studying the Sky

How often have you gazed into the night-time sky and wondered what the stars are, how far away they are, and how the vast universe in which we live came into being? Astronomy, the scientific study of the heavens, attempts to answer these fascinating and fundamental questions. With the help of giant telescopes on Earth and satellites in space, astronomers have discovered the true nature of stars and planets, and have pieced together much of the history of the known universe. They can now make limited predictions about what may happen in the future: how the Sun and Earth may die, and what will be the eventual fate of the universe.

Astronomy is both the oldest and the youngest of the sciences. Records of events in the sky go back to the birth of writing, thousands of years BC, while a growing number of people believe that monuments, such as Stonehenge, England, embody an advanced astronomical knowledge, because they are aligned on the rising and setting points of the Sun and Moon. In recent times, the advent of the space age has allowed astronomers to get their first clear views of the heavens, unobscured by the dense and turbulent blanket of the Earth's atmosphere, and even to gain on-the-spot views of our close celestial neighbours, the Moon and planets.

However, while the impressive technological aids of the modern professional astronomer have revolutionized our knowledge of the space around us, for the countless amateur astronomers in each country who scan the sky with binoculars or telescope each clear night, the basic lure of the stars remains – the same lure that has always turned man's eyes and imagination skywards.

Although the stars at first sight seem to be countless, on even a dark, clear night there are no more than about 2000 stars at any one time visible to the naked eye. Long before the birth of Christ, imaginative astronomers grouped the stars into patterns known as constellations, representing mythical gods and heroes. Astronomers continue this convenient tradition today; there are a total of eighty-eight constellations which cover the entire sky.

Astronomical alignments at Stonehenge. The first part of Stonehenge on Salisbury Plain, Wiltshire, England was constructed about 2500 BC. It consisted of a circular bank and a ring of fifty-six holes, called the Aubrey holes, plus the heelstone. Four stones (here marked A, B, C, D) on the ring of Aubrey holes produce a rectangle, the short sides of which point to the direction of midsummer sunrise and midwinter sunset, while the long sides point to the most southerly rising and the most northerly setting of the Moon. The famous central ring of standing stones was constructed much later, and has no apparent astronomical significance.

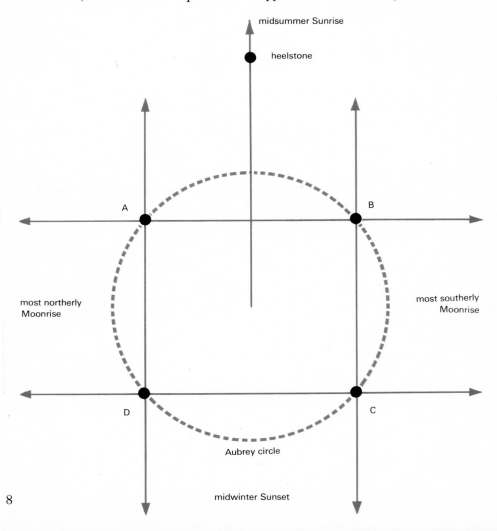

midsummer Sunrise

heelstone

A

B

most northerly Moonrise

most southerly Moonrise

D

C

Aubrey circle

midwinter Sunset

Stonehenge is a monument on Salisbury Plain, England, which some astronomers believe was used as an observatory to follow the motion of the Sun and Moon around the sky during the year, possibly with the intention of predicting eclipses.

Overleaf
Chinese star chart of around 1700.

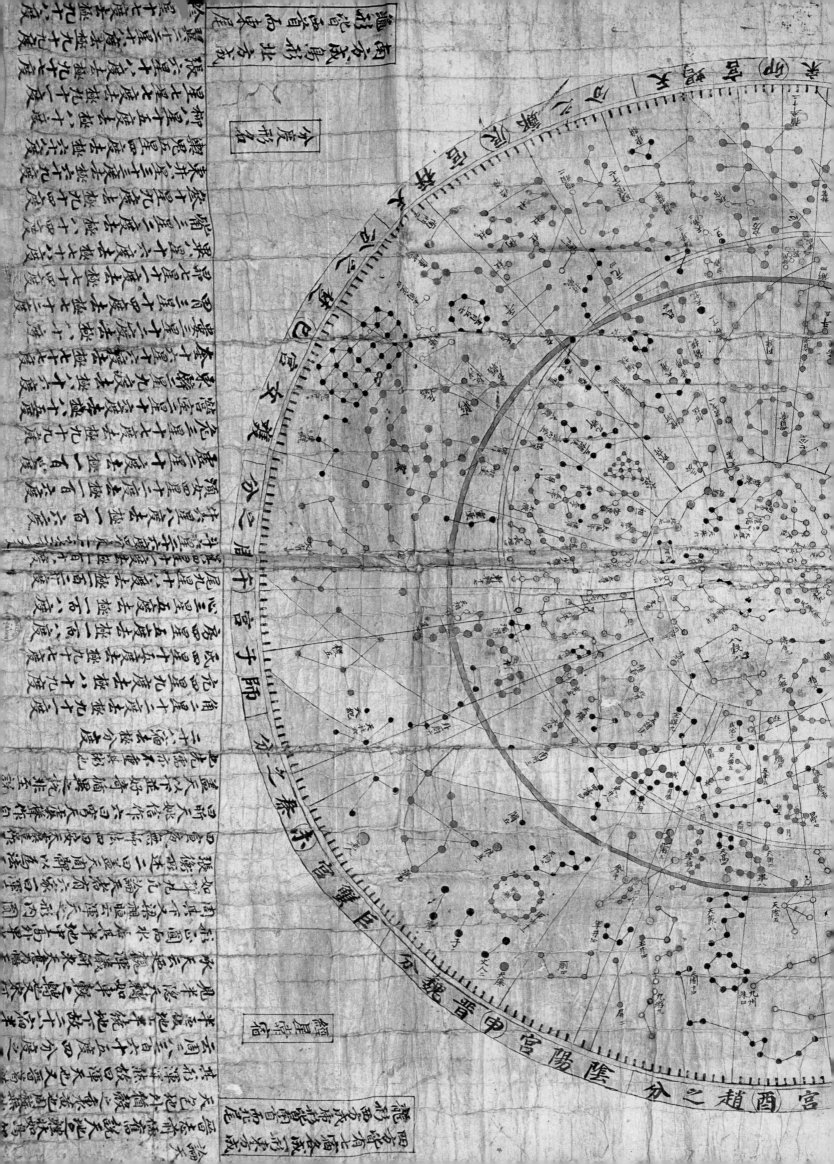

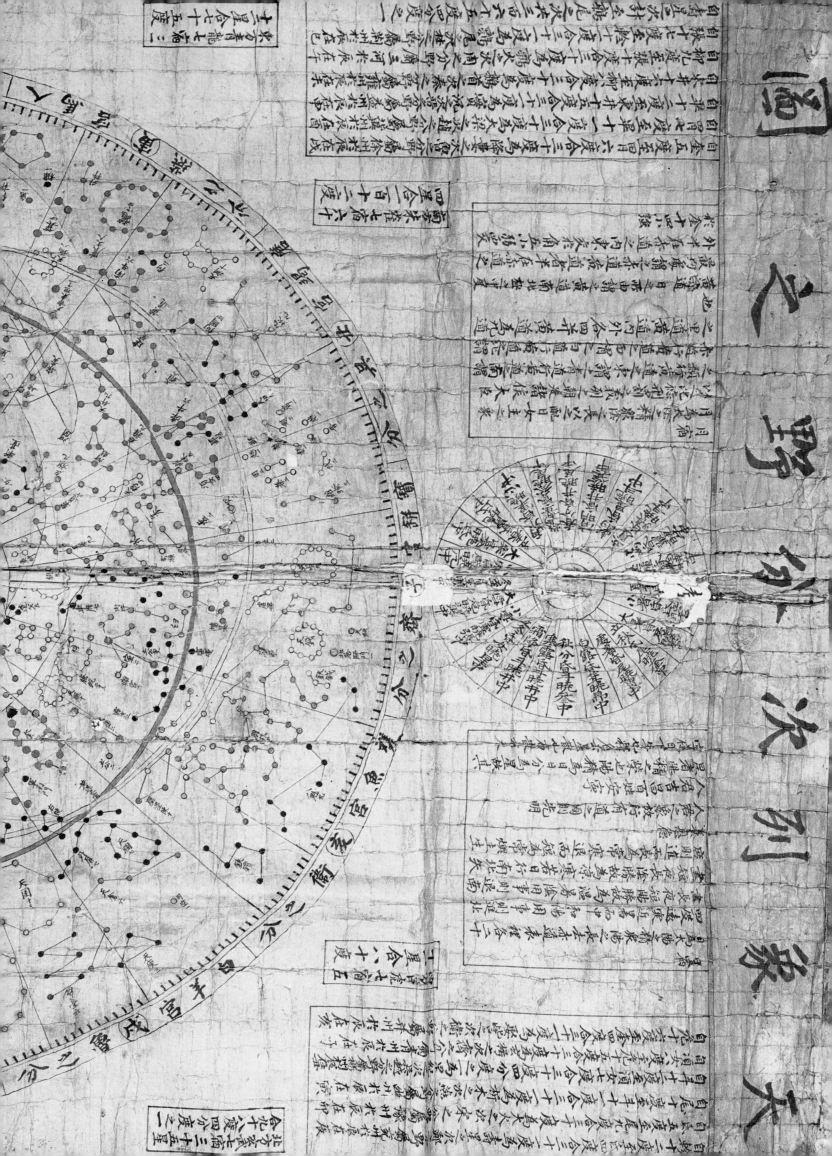

The stars visible each night change with the seasons as the Earth orbits the Sun. For instance, the magnificent constellation of Orion, the hunter, is easily visible in the early evening during December, January, and February, but by June it is invisible from Earth, having passed behind the Sun. The aspect of the skies also changes with one's latitude on Earth – the altitude of the north or south celestial pole above the horizon depends on how far north or south of the equator you are.

The major constellations of the northern and southern skies are shown on the two maps on the facing page. To begin an interest in astronomy needs no optical aid at all, other than your own eyes: familiarizing yourself with the appearance of the heavens is the first important step. Dedicated amateurs, using nothing more elaborate than binoculars, cameras, or their eyes alone, have been able to feed professional astronomers important information on stars that erupt into prominence

of fluctuate in brightness. Amateurs also carefully observe the tiny particles of interplanetary debris that burn up in the Earth's atmosphere to become the brilliant streaks known as meteors. Space-age amateurs help track the orbits of satellites as they orbit the Earth.

We now know that stars are glowing balls of gas like our own Sun, only much farther away – so far, in fact, that their light takes years to reach us. However, to a casual observer, the stars appear to lie relatively close to us on a dome encompassing the Earth and, until a few centuries ago, most people believed that this really was the case. They thought that the dome of stars rotated around the Earth once each day, along with the Sun, Moon and planets. This view, known as the geocentric theory, assumed that the Earth was the centre of the universe. Astronomers of the time did not know the true nature of the stars, nor did they realize that planets are non-luminous bodies like the Earth

that shine by reflecting sunlight. These facts did not emerge until after the invention of the telescope in the seventeenth century.

Ancient notions of the universe, before the rise of Greek civilization, were admittedly fanciful. The peoples of the Middle East, thousands of years before Christ, pictured the Earth as a flat slab surrounded by water. To the ancient Egyptians, the sky was the star-studded body of the goddess Nut; the Sun god Ra sailed in a boat across the sky each day, while the planets voyaged out in their own boats at night. In the Hindu view, our world was carried on the backs of four elephants.

Perhaps the first true astronomer was the Greek Anaximander (c.610–c.546 BC) who realized that the Earth's surface is curved, not flat; he pictured it as a short cylinder suspended at the centre of the universe. The Greek mathematician Pythagoras, in the sixth century BC, made the first recorded suggestion that the Earth is a sphere, an idea that would

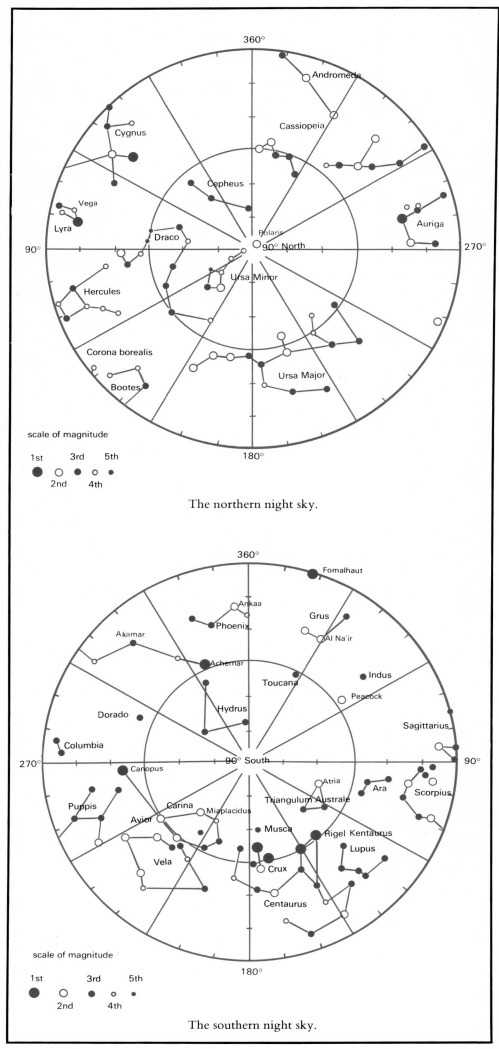

The northern night sky.

The southern night sky.

have seemed quite sensible to navigators and other travellers who observed how the altitude of the pole star changed as they moved north or south. Pythagoras believed that the Sun, Moon and the five wandering 'stars' known as planets moved around the Earth on crystalline spheres, each of which made its own heavenly music as it turned – the so-called music of the spheres.

Pythagoras's concern with musical harmony may have outweighed his regard for strict astronomical accuracy, but his concept of a spherical Earth gained widespread acceptance. In one of the great achievements of the ancient world, the Greek scientist Eratosthenes, in about 240 BC, calculated the circumference of the Earth to be 40 000 kilometres (25 000 miles), to an accuracy of a few per cent, by observing the different altitude of the Sun (caused by the Earth's curvature) seen from two places in Egypt of known distance apart. It is surprising that Columbus, 1 700 years later, should have believed

How Eratosthenes measured the Earth. When the Sun appeared overhead at Syene in Egypt, at Alexandria some distance due north the Sun was about 7° from the vertical, or one-fiftieth of a circle. Therefore, the circumference of the Earth must be fifty times the distance from Alexandria to Syene. Eratosthenes thus calculated that the Earth's circumference is the equivalent of approximately 40 000 kilometres (24 800 miles), very nearly the correct value.

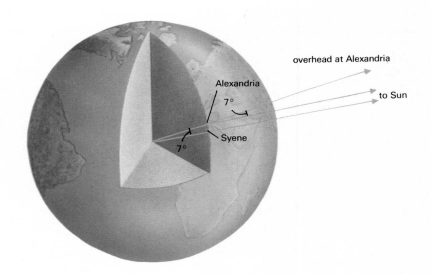

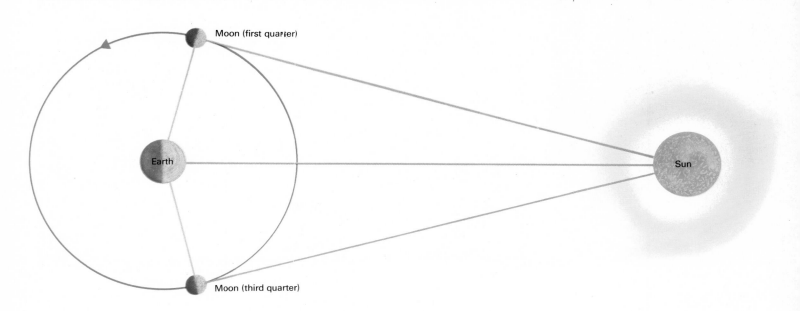

Aristarchus sought to measure the relative distances of the Sun and Moon from Earth by simple trigonometry. When the Moon is half illuminated, the angle between the Earth, Moon and Sun is a right angle. By measuring the angle between the Moon, Earth and Sun, Aristarchus estimated that the Sun is twenty times farther away from Earth than the Moon. Actually this value is too small because he measured the angle inaccurately.

How Aristarchus estimated the relative sizes of the Sun and Moon.
The size of the Earth's shadow at the distance of the Moon could be estimated at lunar eclipses to be 2·66 times the Moon's diameter. Having already estimated the relative distances of the Sun and Moon, Aristarchus could complete a scale drawing of the Moon, Earth, and Sun. His result for the size of the Moon was nearly right, but he underestimated the size of the Sun because he thought it was closer than it really is.

Copernicus's heliocentric (Sun-centred) theory as depicted in a book of 1661, showing the Moon orbiting the Earth and the four main satellites of Jupiter discovered by Galileo.

that the Earth was only about half its actual size. This error is one reason why Columbus had trouble finding sponsorship for his proposed trans-atlantic voyage. Those to whom he first turned probably knew the size of the Earth better than he did.

In the third century BC, the Greek astronomer Aristarchus estimated the relative distances of the Sun and Moon, and calculated their sizes in relation to the Earth. Aristarchus was nearly right in his estimate that the Moon is one-third the diameter of the Earth – actually it is 3 476 kilometres (2 160 miles) in diameter against the Earth's 12,756 kilometres (7 926 miles). However, his estimate that the Sun is seven times the Earth's size and lies twenty times farther away than the Moon was far short of the mark – the Sun is actually 109 Earth diameters, and lies at a distance of 149 million kilometres (93 million miles) as against the Moon's 384 400 kilometres (239 000 miles).

Despite this serious underestimate, Aristarchus had at least shown that the Sun was clearly bigger than the Earth, which was his justification for proposing that the Sun was the centre of the universe, with all other bodies revolving around it rather than around the Earth. This so-called heliocentric or Sun-centred theory did not gain favour among Arist-archus's contemporaries, and was not revived until the time of Copern-icus, 1 800 years later.

Scientists preferred instead to follow the word of the outstanding Greek philosopher Aristotle (384– 322 BC), who denied that the Earth moved in space or even that it turned upon its axis. He asserted that the Earth was immovably fixed at the centre of the universe, although he did agree that it was a sphere. To Aristotle, the heavens were perfect and unchanging and, like Pythagoras before him, he held that the Sun, Moon and planets moved around the Earth on crystalline spheres. Unfor-tunately, detailed observations had shown that the movement of the celestial bodies was not uniform, so Aristotle devised a complex system involving a total of 55 spheres rota-ting at different speeds in an attempt

15

to account for these irregular motions. This cumbersome and unconvincing scheme was later abandoned.

By common consent, the greatest of all Greek astronomers was Hipparchus who, in the second century BC, made a catalogue of 850 stars which was still in use by astronomers in the Middle Ages. Hipparchus divided the stars in his catalogue into six classes of brightness, called magnitudes. First-magnitude stars were the brightest, while sixth-magnitude stars were the faintest visible to the naked eye. Astronomers use a refined version of this magnitude system today.

Hipparchus observed the motions of the Sun and Moon as accurately as his simple sighting instruments would allow. His results led to improved accuracy in the prediction of eclipses, which happen when the Moon blocks off the Sun's light from Earth (a solar eclipse) or passes into the Earth's shadow (a lunar eclipse). Hipparchus abandoned Aristotle's clumsy system of multiple spheres

and showed instead that the Sun's motion could be accounted for by a circle with the centre slightly offset from the Earth. He was, however, unable to account accurately for the motion of the Moon by such a simple system, and he left the even more difficult problem of the motion of the planets untouched.

The final landmark in Greek astronomy was Ptolemy (*c*.100–*c*.178 AD), who wrote a major astronomical encyclopedia now known by its Arabic name of the *Almagest* (the greatest), much of it based on the work of Hipparchus. In the *Almagest*, Ptolemy attempted to summarize all of the preceding Greek astronomy and to produce a final description of the motions of celestial bodies around the Earth. He adopted the idea that the basic orbits of the Moon and planets were circles whose centres were offset from the Earth; to account for added irregularities in the objects' motions he proposed that they also traced out smaller circles, known as epicycles, as they moved around the circumference of

their orbital path. Although this system of offset circles and epicycles described celestial motions far better than anything that had gone before, in retrospect it seems hardly more likely than the multiple crystalline spheres of Aristotle. Ptolemy, like all Greek astronomers, embraced the assumption that the heavens were perfect, and that only the 'perfect' shape of the sphere or the circle were good enough for the motions of celestial bodies.

For nearly 1500 years after Ptolemy, astronomy in Europe entered a period of total eclipse – the Dark Ages. The knowledge of the Greeks passed into Arab hands, where it was preserved and eventually passed back to Europe through the Arab conquest of Spain. Arab astronomy bequeathed us the popular names of many stars such as Aldebaran, Altair and Algol.

Astronomy was eventually shaken out of its dormancy during the Renaissance by a Polish monk, Nicolaus Copernicus (1473–1543). By this time it had become clear that there were serious discrepancies between the observed positions of the planets and those predicted by the geocentric theory of Ptolemy. Against the tide of accepted astronomical thought, Copernicus turned back to the Sun-centred or heliocentric theory originated by Aristarchus. He believed that in doing so he could produce a simpler and more accurate description of the movements of the heavenly bodies. On this theory, a planet's distance from the Sun depended on its speed of movement in the sky, from quicksilver Mercury at the nearest out to sluggish Saturn, the farthest planet then known. If Mercury and Venus orbited closer to the Sun than Earth, this would explain why they never appeared far from the Sun in the sky. The occasional backward loops taken by planets such as Mars could be readily explained by the Earth catching up and overtaking more distant planets on their larger and slower orbits around the Sun.

Copernicus published his theory in 1543, the year of his death, in a book entitled *On the Revolutions of the Celestial Spheres*. However, the theory suffered one major flaw – it still described the orbits of the planets in terms of complex combi-

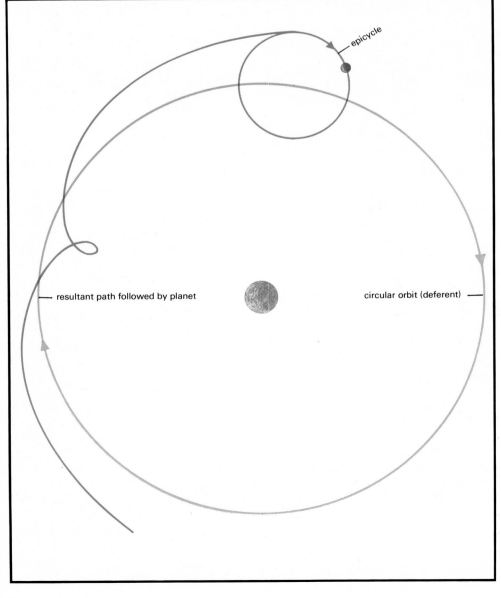

— resultant path followed by planet   circular orbit (deferent) —

epicycle

To explain the somewhat erratic observed motions of the planets, astronomers from Ptolemy onwards used a complex combination of large circles and smaller circles, known as deferents and epicycles.

nations of circles and epicycles. In many ways, therefore, it seemed little improvement on the theory of Ptolemy. One criticism levelled against the heliocentric theory was that if the Earth really did move then the positions of the stars should seem to change during the year, in the same way as a tree shifts against the background as one moves around a field. Copernicus answered this objection by arguing (correctly as we now know) that the stars must be exceptionally distant compared with the Sun; but at the time his argument seemed unconvincing.

A new attack on the problem of planetary motion was made by the Danish astronomer Tycho Brahe (1546–1601), the last great observer of the pre-telescopic era. Tycho realized that all existing tables of planetary motions were inaccurate, even those of Copernicus, and so he set out to make precise observations from which new theories of planetary motion could be derived. Tycho's observations overthrew many cherished beliefs about the heavens. He proved that a new star which flared up temporarily in the sky in 1572 lay far off in space, thus contradicting the Greek dogma that the heavens were unchanging and that all such transient events originated in the Earth's atmosphere. (The remains of this exploded star, known

Left
Nicolaus Copernicus, the Polish astronomer who believed that the Earth was an ordinary planet orbiting the Sun.

Right
Earth-centred view of the universe according to the Greek astronomer and geographer Ptolemy, as depicted in a book of 1661.

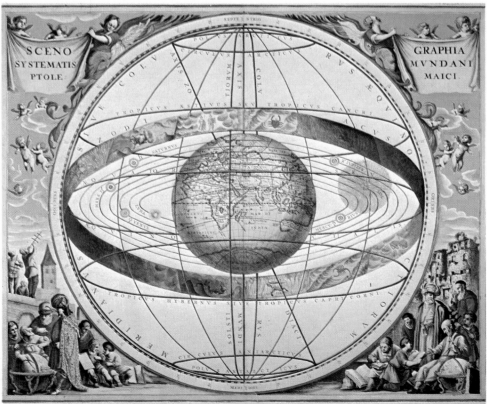

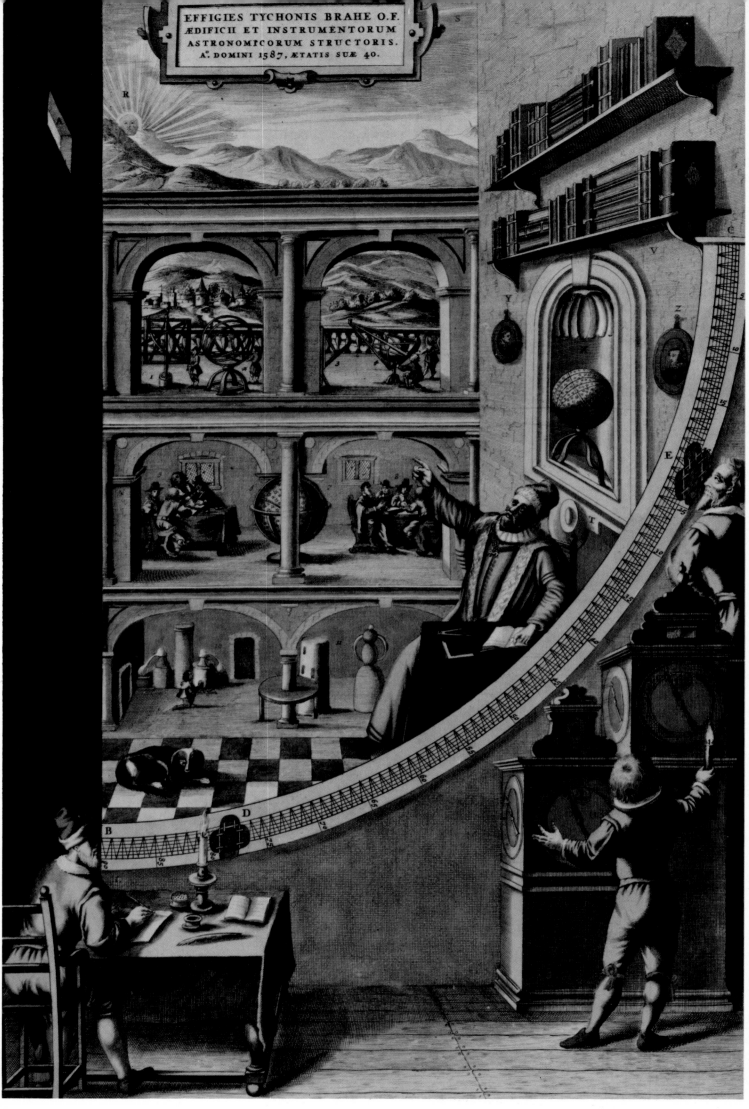

EFFIGIES TYCHONIS BRAHE O.F.
ÆDIFICII ET INSTRUMENTORUM
ASTRONOMICORUM STRUCTORIS.
Aᵒ. DOMINI 1587, ÆTATIS SUÆ 40.

as Tycho's supernova, are still detectable by astronomers today.) Five years later, Tycho showed that the bright comet of 1577 moved among the orbits of the planets, thus finally shattering any remaining faith in the Greek concept of crystalline spheres.

Tycho never accepted the Copernican theory; instead he developed his own compromise theory in which the planets orbited the Sun while the Sun and stars orbited the Earth. He took as his assistant a young German mathematician, Johannes Kepler (1571–1630), to whom he bequeathed his observations in the hope that Kepler might prove the Tychonic view of the heavens. After six years of calculations, Kepler discovered the truth about the planets' orbits – but rather than supporting Tycho, his results eventually established the Copernican theory.

Kepler found that the planets travel around the Sun not in complex combinations of circular motions but along simple curves called ellipses. The planets speed up and slow down along their elliptical orbits as they move nearer to or farther from the Sun. Kepler later discovered a formula that links a planet's distance from the Sun with the time taken to complete its orbit. Kepler's laws of planetary motion are at the heart of our modern understanding of the solar system.

Even as Kepler published his discovery about the shape of planetary orbits in 1609, other events were happening that would lead to the triumphant acceptance of the Copernican theory. In that same year, the Italian scientist Galileo Galilei (1564–1642) heard of the invention

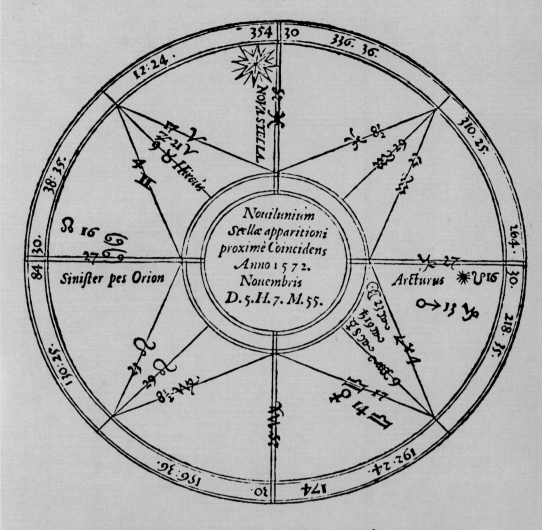

Left
Tycho Brahe in his observatory on the island of Ven between Denmark and Sweden, making observations with a quadrant instrument attached to a wall. In the engraving on the wall are shown other instruments used by Tycho.

Below
Johannes Kepler showed that the planets orbit the Sun in elliptical orbits, like the shape of a squashed circle. A planet moves faster when it is nearer the Sun, so that it takes the same time to move from A to B as from C to D.

Above
Tycho's drawing of the position of the 1572 supernova in Cassiopeia.

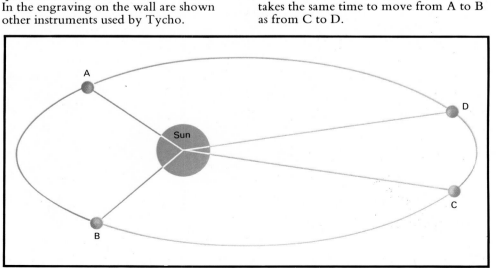

of the telescope and decided to construct one for himself. (A Dutch optician, Hans Lippershey, c.1570–c.1619, is usually credited with the invention of the telescope, although other people experimenting with lenses almost certainly discovered the principle before he did.) The telescope Galileo built is of the type known as a refractor, which uses a lens called an object glass to collect light and focus it so that it can be magnified by another lens known as the eyepiece. Galileo's best telescope had an object glass of only 44 millimetres (1·75 inches) aperture and magnified objects thirty-three times. Optically it was crude – a modern pair of binoculars will show the sky as clearly as Galileo saw it – but the detail he was able to see with this relatively primitive instrument created a revolution in scientific theories.

First of all, Galileo found that the surface of the Moon was pockmarked with craters – further proof that the objects in the heavens were not perfect as the Greeks had claimed. Turning to the Milky Way, the hazy band of light that crosses the sky, Galileo could see faint stars through his telescope that were invisible to the naked eye. This was an indication that the universe was infinitely vaster than the traditional views of astron-

Right
In a simple refracting telescope, here shown partly in cutaway, the object lens collects light and focuses it so that it can be magnified by a smaller lens, the eyepiece. In practice, for best optical results the object glass and eyepiece are usually made of several lenses combined.

Below
Tycho Brahe's system of the universe placed the Earth at the centre, orbited by the Sun around which the other planets circled.

Opposite
Galileo Galilei, the Italian scientist, whose observations with the telescope helped confirm the theory of Copernicus that the Earth orbited the Sun.

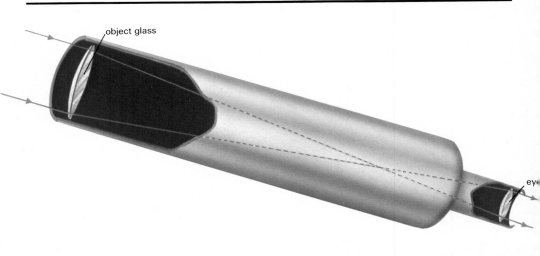

object glass

eye

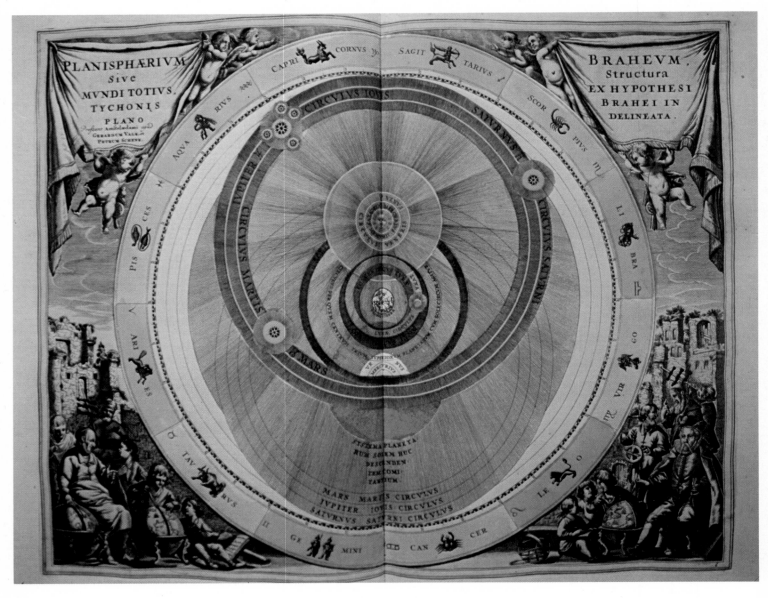

V. l'incis. al vol. LXIX, n. 104

Galileo

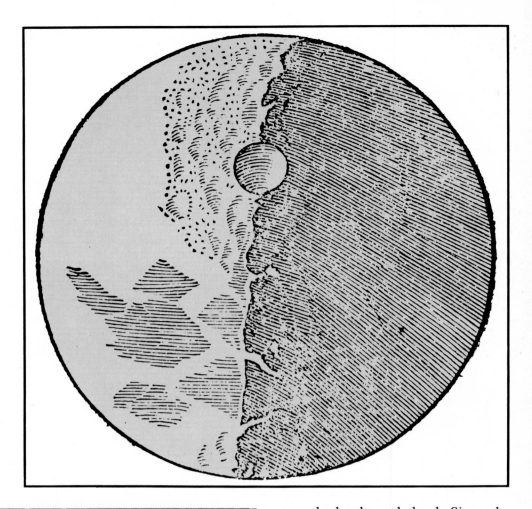

Right
Galileo's drawing of the Moon, reproduced in his book *Sidereus Nuncius* of 1610, showed that the Moon had mountains and valleys, and was not perfect as the Greeks had maintained.

Below
Isaac Newton, whose laws of gravity explained why the planets orbited the Sun.

Opposite
The first reflecting telescope, built by Isaac Newton in 1668, had a mirror 5 centimetres (2 inches) in diameter.

SIR ISAAC NEWTON
*Painted by
Sir Godfrey Kneller.
1702*

omy had acknowledged. Since the stars remained as points of light in his telescope they must indeed be very far away, as Copernicus had maintained. Most significantly of all, Galileo saw for the first time that the planet Venus went through a cycle of phases similar to those of the Moon, and the only way that Venus could show changing phases was if it orbited the Sun. Here was observational verification of the theory of Copernicus. Further direct support for Copernicus came from Galileo's discovery of the four bright moons of Jupiter, which he likened to a smaller version of the planets orbiting the Sun.

The new view of the heavens given by the telescope, coming hard on the heels of Kepler's theoretical breakthrough, meant that the old Earth-centred view of the heavens was gone forever. Even the efforts of the Catholic church, which put Galileo on trial and made him publicly reject the heliocentric theory, could not prevent the overthrow of traditional concepts of astronomy and man's place in the universe. By 1687, when Sir Isaac Newton (1642–1727) published his theory of gravity which explained in physical terms why planets orbited the Sun as they do, there could no longer be any doubt that the heliocentric theories were correct.

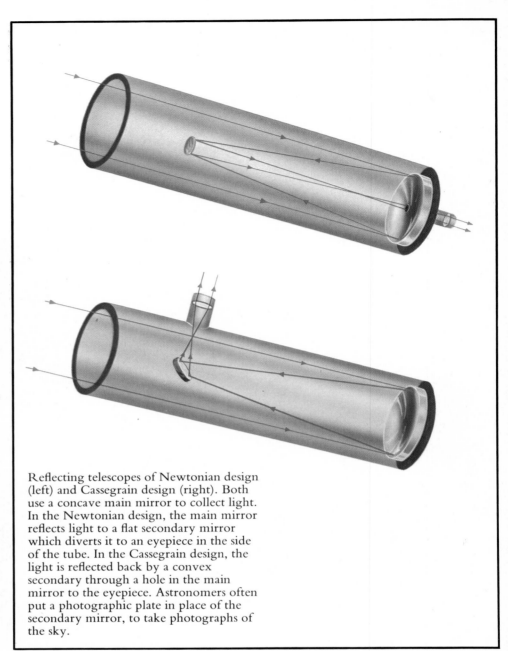

Sir William Herschel's great telescope, 12·2 metres (40 feet) long, with a mirror 122 centimetres (48 inches) in diameter. It was the largest telescope in the world when built in 1789.

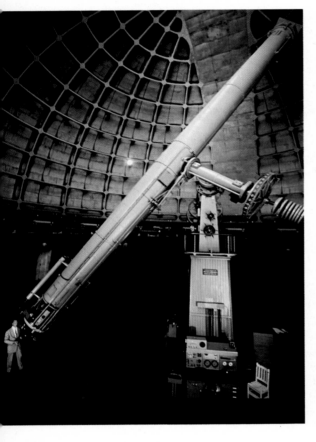

The 91-centimetre (36-inch) telescope at the Lick Observatory, the second largest refractor in the world.

Reflecting telescopes of Newtonian design (left) and Cassegrain design (right). Both use a concave main mirror to collect light. In the Newtonian design, the main mirror reflects light to a flat secondary mirror which diverts it to an eyepiece in the side of the tube. In the Cassegrain design, the light is reflected back by a convex secondary through a hole in the main mirror to the eyepiece. Astronomers often put a photographic plate in place of the secondary mirror, to take photographs of the sky.

Newton advanced astronomy in another way in 1668 when he built a telescope of the kind known as a reflector, which uses mirrors instead of lenses to collect and focus light. Reflectors soon caught on, both in Newton's design and in other designs originated by the Scotsman James Gregory (who in 1663 was the first to propose the principle of the reflecting telescope, although he never built one) and a French physicist named Cassegrain. Mankind's view of the universe was further expanded in 1781 when the English astronomer William Herschel (1738–1822), using a reflector of 15-centimetre (6-inch) aperture, discovered a previously unknown planet, Uranus. Until that time the solar system had been thought to end with Saturn, which is the farthest planet from the Sun visible to the naked eye. Herschel's discovery of distant Uranus doubled the size of the known solar system and awakened astronomers to the possibility of still more planets. In 1846 and 1930 two more planets, Neptune and Pluto, were discovered, both as the result of deliberate searches. Using reflectors up to 122-centimetre (48-inch) aperture, Herschel went on to make the most thorough surveys of the starry sky. His studies convinced him that the stars were not arranged uniformly in space, but that they were concentrated into an irregular lens-shape, with the Sun at or near the hub; where we look along the main thickness of stars we see the Milky Way. Thus, although the Earth had been displaced from its position as centre of the universe, the Sun was now visualized as nearly central in a galaxy of stars which was presumed to constitute the entire universe.

Mirrors of that early era were made of a shiny metal alloy of copper and tin which tarnished and had to be regularly repolished. During the nineteenth century, telescope mirrors

View of Herschels, Forty foot reflecting Telescope.

began to be made, as they are today, of glass coated with a reflective layer of silver or aluminium, which provides a much brighter image than the old-fashioned metal mirrors. Whereas lenses had to be made of clear, flawless glass accurately figured on both sides, mirrors were not transparent and had to be figured on one surface only. Therefore, mirrors were much cheaper to make than lenses and, because a mirror can be supported underneath to stop it sagging, they could be made much larger than the lenses. This is important because a telescope's most vital statistic is actually its aperture, not its magnification: the wider the aperture the more light it collects and thus the fainter the objects it can see. Today, astronomers mostly use their telescopes either as giant telephoto lenses to take long-exposure photographs of faint objects in the sky, or to collect light for analysis by subsidiary instruments such as spectro-

scopes. Spectroscopic analysis of an object's light can reveal an amazing amount of information, including its composition, and is one of the most important techniques of the astronomer.

The advantages of cheapness and potential size eventually proved decisive for the popularity of reflectors. No refractors were ever made larger than the 91-centimetre (36-inch) of Lick Observatory and the 1-metre (40-inch) of Yerkes Observatory, which were completed by the American firm of Alvan Clark and Sons in 1888 and 1897 respectively. Since then, all the world's largest telescopes have been reflectors.

The modern era of large reflectors sited in the clear air of high mountains began in 1908 when the American astronomer George Ellery Hale (1868–1938) established the 1·5-metre (60-inch) reflector on top of Mount Wilson in California, 1 742 metres (5 705 feet) high. With this

telescope, the American astronomer Harlow Shapley (1885–1972) made a discovery as momentous in its own way as the theory of Copernicus – Shapley found that our Sun lies not at the centre of our galaxy but about two-thirds of the way to the edge. Our galaxy, which contains approximately 100 000 million stars, is 100 000 light years in diameter – that is to say, light travelling at 300 000 kilometres (186 000 miles) per second takes 100 000 years to cross it.

Hale went on to organize the construction of an even bigger telescope, the Mount Wilson 2·5-metre (100-inch) reflector opened in 1917, which provided more revolutionary discoveries. With this giant eye, Edwin Hubble (1889–1953) discovered that other galaxies exist outside our own, and that they seemed to be receding from us at speeds that increased with their distance, as though the whole universe were expanding. This was the starting point for modern theories

Above
The 5-metre (200-inch) reflector on Mount Palomar in California.

Right
Dome of the 4-metre (158-inch) reflector on Kitt Peak, Arizona.

of cosmology, discussed in more detail in the concluding chapter.

There are now many reflectors throughout the world of 2·5-metre aperture or above. The most famous is the 5-metre (200-inch) Hale reflector, situated 1 706 metres (5 597 feet) high on Mount Palomar, California, opened in 1948. This was the world's largest reflector until the opening in 1976 of the Soviet 6-metre (236-inch) reflector at Zelenchukskaya in the Caucasus mountains. Other large reflectors are at Kitt Peak, Arizona, and Cerro Tololo, Chile (both 4 metres, 158 inches); Siding Spring, New South Wales (3·9 metres, 153 inches); and the European Southern Observatory, Chile (3·6 metres, 142 inches).

Objects in space do not emit just visible light; they also give out radiation at longer and shorter wavelengths, from radio waves to X-rays, that are invisible to the eye. Since World War II, astronomers have been opening up new windows on the heavens to study these other wavelengths. Major new advances have come through radioastronomy, which detects long-wavelength radiation invisible to the eye. An American radio engineer, Karl Jansky (1905–1950), accidentally detected the first radio noise from the galaxy in 1932 while searching for sources of noise on radio-telephone transmissions. Jansky's discovery was followed up by the radio ham Grote Reber (b. 1911) but it was not until after the War that radioastronomy began to flourish. The discoveries of modern radioastronomy have led scientists to the conclusion that the universe is evolving from a gigantic explosion known as the 'Big Bang', which occurred perhaps 20 000 million years ago, as discussed in the final chapter.

Most radio telescopes work rather like reflecting telescopes. A large reflector panel collects radiation and focuses it to a point where it is detected and amplified electronically. The output from radio telescopes is usually stored on magnetic tape. Because radio waves are so much longer than light waves, radio telescopes have to be much bigger than optical telescopes to see the sky in as much detail. In some cases, radioastronomers electronically combine the signal from a line of individual dishes to synthesize the view of the sky that would be seen by one enormous radio dish.

The largest, fully steerable radio dish in the world is the 100-metre (328-foot) telescope of the Effelsberg radio observatory near Bonn, West Germany. The largest single dish in the world is 305 metres (1 000 feet) in diameter at Arecibo, Puerto Rico, slung in a natural hollow between the mountains. It cannot be steered, but scans the sky overhead as the

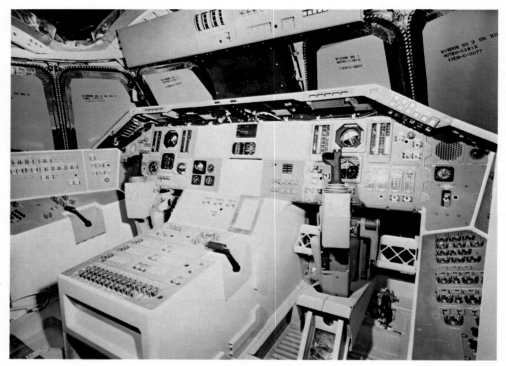

Left
Flight deck of the Space Shuttle orbiter, which two astronauts will fly back to Earth from orbit to land on a runway like a normal aircraft.

Below
America's Skylab space station in orbit around the Earth. The windmill-like arms are the solar cells, which turn sunlight into electricity, attached to the Apollo telescope mount, which contained a set of instruments for observing the Sun.

Right
The 100-metre (328-foot) dish at Effelsberg, near Bonn, West Germany, is the world's largest fully steerable radio telescope.

Earth spins. On the plains near Socorro, New Mexico, radioastronomers are constructing a remarkable instrument known as the Very Large Array. When completed in 1981, the output from its twenty-seven movable antennae, arranged in three arms like a Y, will be combined to give a view of the sky equivalent to that from a single dish 27 kilometres (17 miles) in diameter.

However, the best view of the sky is obtained by observing from orbit. In the 1980s a 2·4-metre (95-inch) reflector, known as the Space Telescope, is due to be launched by the Space Shuttle. Above the blurring effect of the Earth's atmosphere, this telescope should see objects up to 100 times fainter, as well as detail ten times smaller, than existing Earth-based telescopes.

There are many wavelengths of radiation that can be studied only from orbit, because they do not penetrate the atmosphere at all, such as ultraviolet rays, X-rays, and γ (gamma) rays. America's Skylab space station, which was manned by three crews in 1973, carried a series of special telescopes to observe the Sun's short-wavelength emissions. An increasing number of satellites are now being launched to study short-wavelength radiation produced by violent processes in the universe, including X-rays that may come from super-hot gas pouring into black holes in space. The opening up of these new windows on the universe seems certain to produce a revolution in science similar to that which followed the invention of the telescope.

During the 1980s astronomers themselves will be able to fly into orbit using telescopes mounted in the European-built Spacelab space station carried in the cargo bay of the American Space Shuttle transporter. What they will find cannot be foreseen, but that is part of the excitement of the discovery of our universe.

Planets

Our Sun, an average star, is surrounded by a family of nine planets and a host of associated debris which together make up what is known as the solar system. The Sun and its family are believed to have been born from the same cloud of gas and dust in space, approximately 4600 million years ago. According to modern views, the formation of planets is a natural by-product of the birth of stars, so that there may be many other planetary systems in space – some of them, perhaps, harbouring life.

The planets grew, it is theorized, from a ring of leftover material around the primitive Sun. In this cloud, atoms of rock and metal were stuck together by collisions until they were big enough to attract one another by their own gravity. Thus, lumps tens or hundreds of kilometres across were produced, which merged into objects many thousands of kilometres in diameter – the planets. Remnants from this sweeping-up process are the lumps of rock and metal known as meteorites which occasionally collide with the Earth.

Meanwhile, the glowing fires of the young Sun were pushing the light gases out of the solar system. Nearest to the Sun, where it was hottest, only the heaviest elements could remain; there, dense, rock-and-metal planets – Mercury, Venus, Earth and Mars – were formed. Farther away from the Sun, where it was colder, the gas giants of the solar system were formed – Jupiter, Saturn, Uranus and Neptune. At the outermost reaches of the solar system, frozen lumps of rock and ice were left – the comets. All remaining gases were blown away by the Sun's heat, dispersing into space. The Sun contains approximately 99·9 per cent of all the mass now remaining in the solar system.

Heat from the decay of radioactive atoms warmed the interiors of the planets, so that light rocks rose to the top, forming a crust. Sufficient heat remains inside the Earth to cause occasional volcanic eruptions. Gases exhaled from the planets' interiors produced atmospheres; much of the gas from volcanoes on Earth is water vapour, which condensed to form the seas. The smallest bodies, such as Mercury, did not have sufficient gravity to retain these gases, and therefore remain airless and waterless.

Mercury. Let us begin a tour of the solar system at this tiny planet, the closest to the Sun. With the possible exception of remote Pluto,

Below
Relative distances of the planets from the Sun (not to scale).

Right
Formation of the solar system. The Sun and the planets were born from a cloud of gas and dust in space which collapsed under the inward pull of its own gravity. The Sun was formed first, surrounded by a doughnut-shaped cloud of material. Collisions between the atoms in this cloud slowly built up solid lumps of material, which coalesced to form the planets. Much of the gas in this cloud around the Sun was blown away into space.

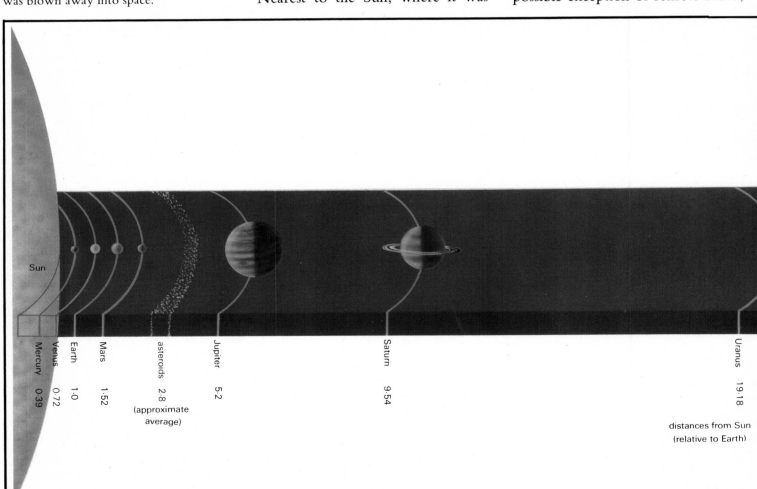

Sun

Mercury 0·39

Venus 0·72

Earth 1·0

Mars 1·52

asteroids 2·8 (approximate average)

Jupiter 5·2

Saturn 9·54

Uranus 19·18

distances from Sun (relative to Earth)

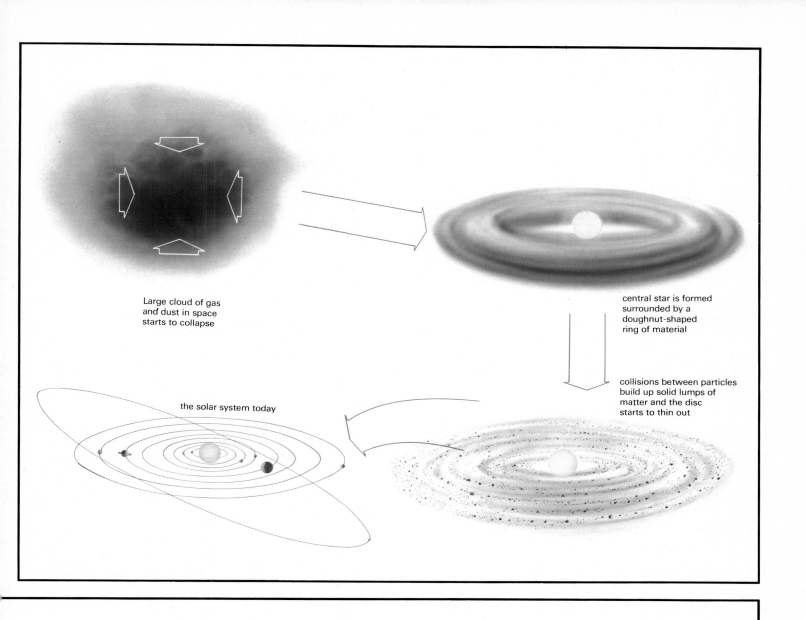

Large cloud of gas
and dust in space
starts to collapse

central star is formed
surrounded by a
doughnut-shaped
ring of material

collisions between particles
build up solid lumps of
matter and the disc
starts to thin out

the solar system today

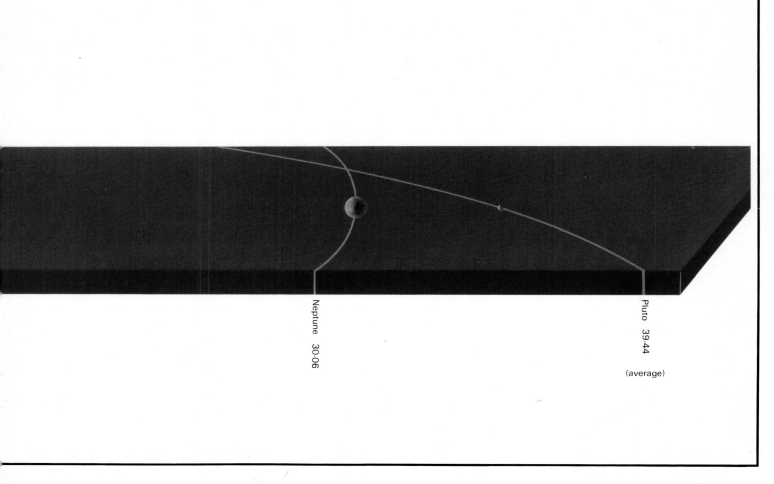

Neptune 30·06

Pluto 39·44

(average)

interplanetary radar, in which a radio beam is bounced off the surface of a planet; the radar reflection reveals both surface detail and the planet's speed of rotation. In the case of Mercury, it revealed that the planet rotates once every 59 days; in other words, it spins one-and-a-half times on its axis every time it orbits the Sun. Therefore, for the Sun to go once around the sky as seen from the planet's surface – say, from one noon to the next – Mercury must complete two orbits, spinning three times on its axis, which takes a total of 176 Earth days.

In 1974, astronomers got their first good look at the planet when the US Mariner 10 space probe sent back photographs which showed that Mercury looks strikingly similar to the Moon. Its rocky surface is pockmarked with giant craters, apparently caused by a bombardment of debris shortly after the formation of the solar system. The largest scar on Mercury is the Caloris Basin, 1 400 kilometres (800 miles) in diameter, which has apparently been flooded by molten lava, like the lowland plains of the Moon. The most recent craters are small, bright pits, often surrounded by bright rays of ejected material. This barren, rugged surface can harbour no form of life. Men will not travel to this forbidding planet for a long time to come.

Venus. This planet, second in line from the Sun was for long even more mysterious than Mercury. Venus orbits the Sun at a distance of 108·2 million kilometres (67·2 million miles), and at its closest can come to within 38 million kilometres (24 million miles) of Earth, nearer than any other planet. Its surface is shrouded from view by an unbroken blanket of white clouds which reflect most of the sunlight that strikes them, so through a telescope the planet appears as little more than a dazzling bright ball that goes through a series of phases as it orbits the Sun every 225 days. At its brightest, Venus is familiar as the morning or evening 'star', outshining all other stars and planets.

Its diameter of 12 100 kilometres (7 520 miles), similar to that of Earth, earned it the nickname 'Earth's twin', but, alas, it has turned out to be very different. During the 1960s, radioastronomers detected radiation from the planet which indicated that its surface temperature was very high. Since then, space probes have parachuted to the surface, confirm-

Mercury, photographed from Mariner 10, with the north pole at the top of the picture. Bright rayed craters are prominent in this view of Mercury.

whose diameter is still not accurately known, Mercury is the smallest planet in the solar system. Its diameter of 4 880 kilometres (3 030 miles) is only 50 per cent larger than our own Moon. For its size, Mercury is very heavy, and is believed to have a core of iron which extends four-fifths of the way to its surface. Fleet-footed Mercury orbits the Sun in a mere 88 days at an average distance of 57·9 million kilometres (36 million miles). From Mercury, the Sun appears two-and-a-half times as large in the sky as it does from Earth; the Sun's

heat is so great that temperatures on the day side of Mercury rise to 350°C, hot enough to melt tin and lead. On the dark side, the temperature of Mercury drops to −170°C.

Mercury is so close to the Sun that it is difficult to see with the naked eye except under the most favourable circumstances. Even telescopes do not show it very clearly, and until recently astronomers knew very little about it. For instance, it was assumed that Mercury spun on its axis in the same time as it took to complete one orbit, so that it kept one face permanently turned towards the Sun, as the Moon does towards the Earth. However, in 1965 astronomers were surprised by results from the new technique of

ing that beneath its clouds Venus resembles hell. Its atmosphere is made up of unbreathable carbon dioxide gas, which at the surface presses down with ninety times the force of the Earth's atmosphere, equivalent to pressures a kilometre deep in the ocean. In addition, the dense atmosphere traps the Sun's heat by what is termed the greenhouse effect, building up a furnace-like surface temperature of 475°C. The bright clouds themselves, which lie at a height of about 80 kilometres (50 miles), are made not of water vapour but of droplets of strong sulphuric acid. Certainly, nothing living is likely to be found on or around Venus – nor is it a welcoming place for astronauts.

During the 1960s, interplanetary radar, which is not blocked by the clouds of Venus, revealed a remarkable fact; the planet rotates in the wrong direction, from east to west instead of from west to east as do the Earth and other planets. The time taken for one rotation, 243 days, is longer than Venus takes to orbit the Sun. How the rotation of Venus was thrown into slow reverse gear remains a puzzle. Another puzzle is that on the Mariner 10 pictures of 1974 the clouds seem to rotate from east to west every 4 days; either there are ultra-fast winds in the upper atmosphere of Venus or the cloud movements shown on the pictures are an illusion. Radar maps of the planet's surface reveal craters up to 300 kilometres (186 miles) in diameter, and a 1 500-kilometre (930-mile)-long crack like the rift valley of Africa.

Venus photographed in ultraviolet light by the Mariner 10 space probe in February 1974, showing swirls in the thick clouds that envelope it.

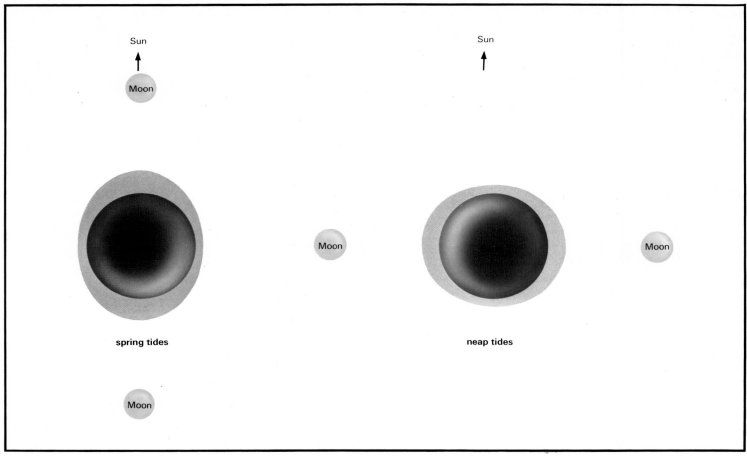

Sun

Moon

Moon

Moon

spring tides

Sun

Moon

neap tides

On-the-spot views from the surface of Venus were returned in 1975
by the Soviet lander craft Venus 9
and Venus 10. Their photographs
showed that Venus is not as gloomy
under its cloud as anticipated – it is
as bright at the surface as on a cloudy
summer's day on Earth. One lander
came down at the foot of a rock
slide, while the other found itself on
a plateau with stony outcrops; the
rocks are similar in composition to
volcanic basalt, like those on the
lunar lowland plains. Internally,
Venus is believed to be like the Earth
– a heavy core surrounded by a
mantle of lighter rock and topped
with a thin crust.

Earth. We live on the third planet
from the Sun: 12 756 kilometres
(7 926 miles) in diameter, lying at an
average distance of 149·6 million
kilometres (93 million miles). Our
Earth, the only planet known to
support life, spins once on its axis
every 24 hours, a period we call the
day, and orbits the Sun once every
365·25 days, which we term a year.
Seen from space, the Earth would be
termed the blue-and-white planet
because of its vast oceans and abundant clouds of water vapour.

Moon. Every 27·3 days we are
orbited by this rocky body, 3 476
kilometres (2 160 miles) in diameter,
whose average distance of 384,400
kilometres (239 000 miles) makes it
by far our closest permanent natural
neighbour. The Moon also takes
27·3 days to rotate once on its axis, so
that it keeps the same face permanently turned towards the Earth.
This state of affairs has come about
because the gravitational pull of the
Earth has decelerated the Moon's
spin into what is termed a 'captured'
rotation. In turn, the Moon's gravity
affects the Earth, producing tides in
the oceans. (The Sun also raises tides
but the Moon, being so much closer,
has a greater effect.) These tides slow
the Earth's rotation by 0·001 seconds
per century. Although this sounds
trivially small, the effect builds up
over long periods; the daily growth
bands of fossil corals reveal that 380
million years ago there were 22 hours
per day, and 400 days in a year.

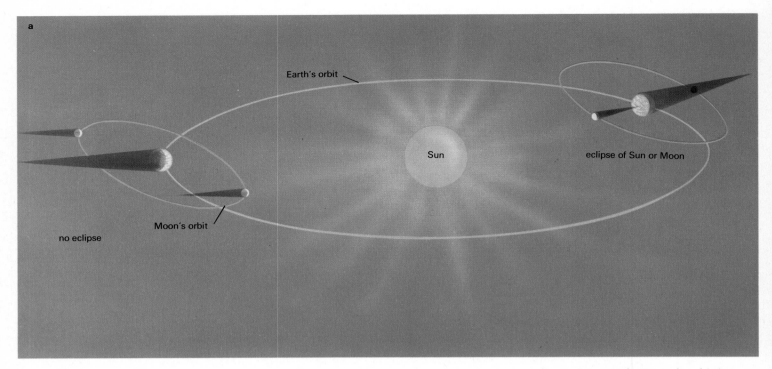

a

Earth's orbit

Sun

eclipse of Sun or Moon

Moon's orbit

no eclipse

Eclipses. Because the Moon's orbit is inclined at 5° to the orbit of the Earth (a), eclipses only happen occasionally when the Moon comes into line with the Sun and Earth; if the Moon's orbit were not so inclined, there would be a solar eclipse at each new Moon, and a lunar eclipse at each full Moon. A total eclipse of the Sun (b) is seen at those places on Earth inside the darkest part of the Moon's shadow, the umbra; in the outer part of the shadow, the penumbra, only a partial eclipse is seen. The amount of partial eclipse depends on whereabouts inside the penumbra the observer stands. At some eclipses, the Moon's umbra falls short of the Earth, so that even at the centre of the umbra the observer sees a ring of sunlight around the Moon; this is termed an annular eclipse, from the Latin word *annulus* meaning ring. Elsewhere in the penumbra, the observer will see a partial eclipse, as before. At a lunar eclipse, the Moon enters the Earth's shadow, as shown in diagram (c).

Left
Phases of the Moon. These occur as the Moon orbits the Earth, so that we see different amounts of its illuminated hemisphere.

Overleaf
Apollo 15 astronaut James B. Irwin stands next to the lunar rover on the Moon's surface, with Mount Hadley in the background.

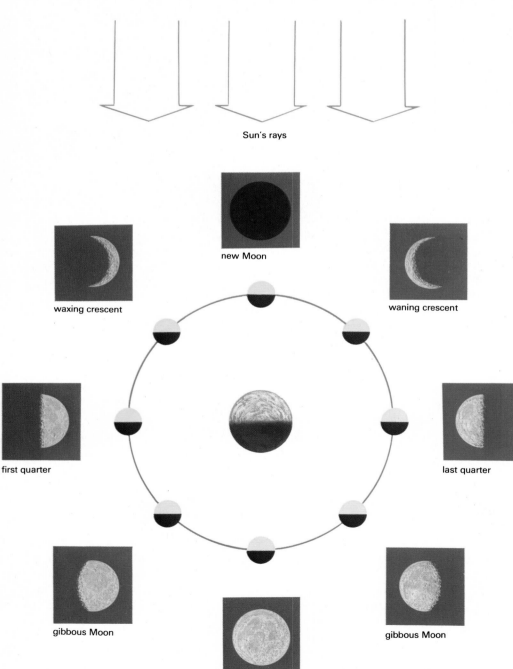

Sun's rays

new Moon

waxing crescent

waning crescent

first quarter

last quarter

gibbous Moon

gibbous Moon

full Moon

Each month, the Moon goes through its familiar cycle of phases from new, through crescent, half, gibbous, to full, and back again. These phases are caused as the Moon orbits the Earth and we see different amounts of its illuminated portion. Since the Moon's path is inclined at 5° to the Earth's orbit around the Sun, the three bodies come in line only occasionally to cause an eclipse. About twice a year the Moon passes in front of the Sun to cause a solar

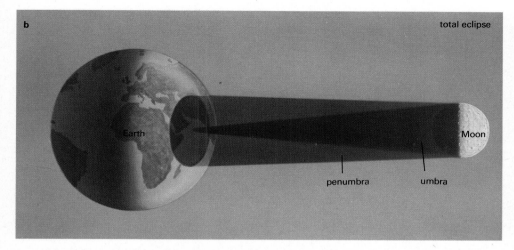

Total eclipse, seen inside the umbra.

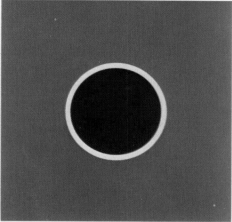

Partial eclipse seen in penumbra.

eclipse; and about as often the Moon passes into the Earth's shadow, producing a lunar eclipse.

Even a casual glance at the Moon with the naked eye shows the dark lowland plains which form the so-called 'man in the Moon'. Galileo named these dark areas *maria*, Latin for seas, because he thought they really did contain water. We now know that the Moon is airless and waterless, but the name has stuck. Binoculars or a small telescope will disclose countless craters pitting the Moon's surface, particularly in the bright lunar highlands. After centuries of controversy, it is now generally accepted that the craters were formed by meteorite impacts, rather than by volcanoes as was once

thought. (There are, however, a few small examples of volcanic activity on the Moon.)

Astronomers have mapped the visible hemisphere of the Moon in increasing detail, naming major formations after famous scientists and, in some cases, historical or mythical characters. The far side of the Moon remained unseen and mysterious until 1959, when it was first photographed by the Soviet probe Luna 3. Following that, a whole series of unmanned American lunar orbiting craft photographed the entire Moon, front and back, in greater detail than ever before. Surprisingly, the Moon's averted hemisphere is quite different in appearance from the side with which we are familiar; instead of large mare areas, it is mostly bright uplands, saturated with craters of all sizes. Evidently, the crust on the Earth-facing hemisphere is thinner, so that the dark lavas could burst through to form the maria.

Now, six Apollo crews have landed on the Moon and brought back 380 kilograms (840 pounds) of rocks. Apollo experiments on the surface and from orbit increased the

Annular eclipse, seen at centre of penumbra.

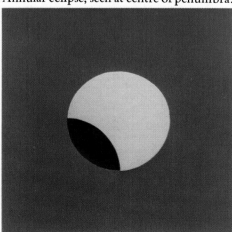

Partial eclipse, seen elsewhere in penumbra.

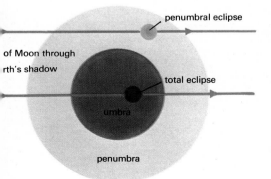

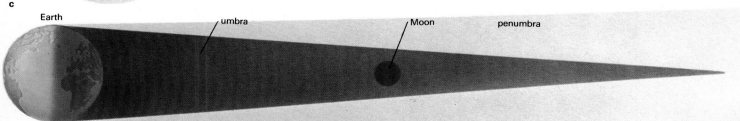

Craters in the rugged highlands of the Moon's far side.

knowledge gained by the first unmanned pathfinder probes, enabling astronomers to piece together a clear picture of the Moon's history. Overall, the Moon is less dense than the Earth. While the Moon rocks are broadly similar to volcanic basalt on Earth, there are subtle differences in composition which set them apart. Old ideas that the Moon split from the Earth have now been abandoned in favour of a separate formation for the Moon, but close enough to the Earth to be tied to it by gravity.

Although the Moon is now cold inside, shortly after its birth it must have been much warmer. The lightest rocks rose to the top, forming a crust, while denser materials settled to the centre, forming a core. For several hundred million years the lunar crust was subjected to a relentless bombardment from debris left over after the solar system's formation. Impact piled upon impact, pulverizing the crust, until the storm abated. Deep basins were dug by the largest impacts, into which molten lava seeped from below between 4 000 million and 3 000 million years

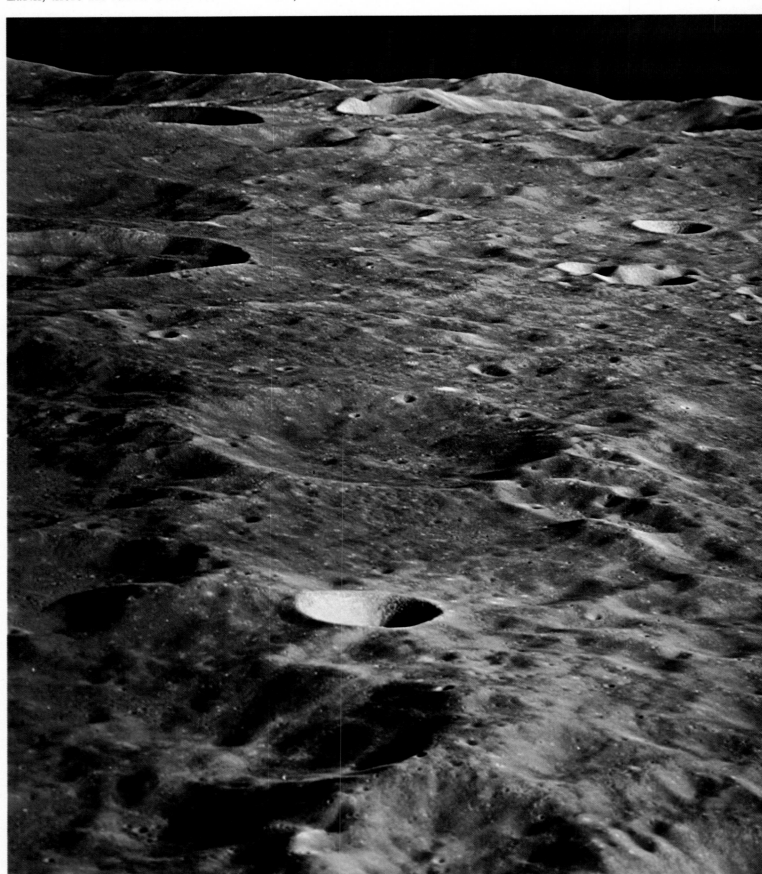

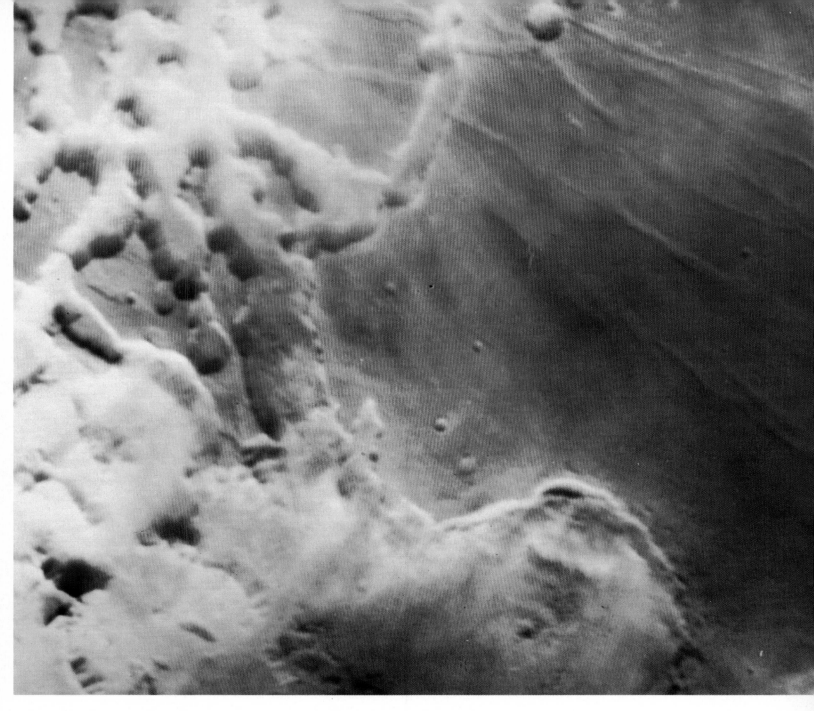

ago to produce the flat, dark maria. During that period on Earth, continents were being built and the first life appeared. Since then, the face of the Moon has been disturbed only by the occasional encounter with a stray meteorite, and a continual peppering by micrometeorites like cosmic hailstones that churn the rocks into fine soil. However, in the next few decades, it will be disturbed when men return to the Moon to set up bases and perhaps to mine its crust for the iron, titanium, magnesium, and other minerals in which it is so rich.

Mars. Fourth in line from the Sun is the planet that was once thought likely to harbour other life – Mars, popularly known as the red planet because of its distinctive colour, now known to be caused by large amounts of reddish-brown iron oxide in its crust. Mars orbits the Sun every 687 days at an average distance of 227·9

million kilometres (141·6 million miles). Although its diameter of 6 787 kilometres (4 217 miles) is only about half that of our home planet, Mars has many superficial similarities with the Earth. For instance, it rotates once every 24·5 hours, giving it a day scarcely longer than our own. It has a thin atmosphere in which clouds form, and two glistening white polar caps that melt during the summer and re-form each winter.

Through a telescope, Mars shows several dark markings that appear greenish in hue by contrast with the bright red deserts surrounding them, and which astronomers once thought might be vegetation. During the close approach between Earth and Mars in 1877, the Italian astronomer, Giovanni Schiaparelli (1835–1910), detected a number of straight markings which he termed *canali*, meaning channels. The word was mistranslated as canals, implying that

Noctis Labyrinthus, taken by Viking Orbiter 1. Bright clouds of water ice can be seen in and around the tributary canyons of this high plateau region of Mars.

they were of artificial construction, which Schiaparelli did not believe. Percival Lowell (1855–1916), a wealthy American astronomer who set up his own observatory at Flagstaff, Arizona, became firmly convinced that the canals were artificial waterways dug by Martians to bring water from the polar caps to irrigate their crops at the equator. Other astronomers failed to see the network of fine lines drawn by Lowell; instead, under the best conditions, the so-called canals seemed to break up into disjointed dots and splodges. The canal controversy was finally laid to rest by the close-up views afforded by space probes, which confirmed that the canals do not exist. Lowell and his followers had been deluded by tricks of the eye.

What the space probes did find were craters like those on the Moon, relics of the sweeping-up process after the formation of the solar system. The probes also found that the atmosphere of Mars was made of carbon dioxide and was far thinner than expected – as thin as the Earth's atmosphere at a height of 32 kilo-

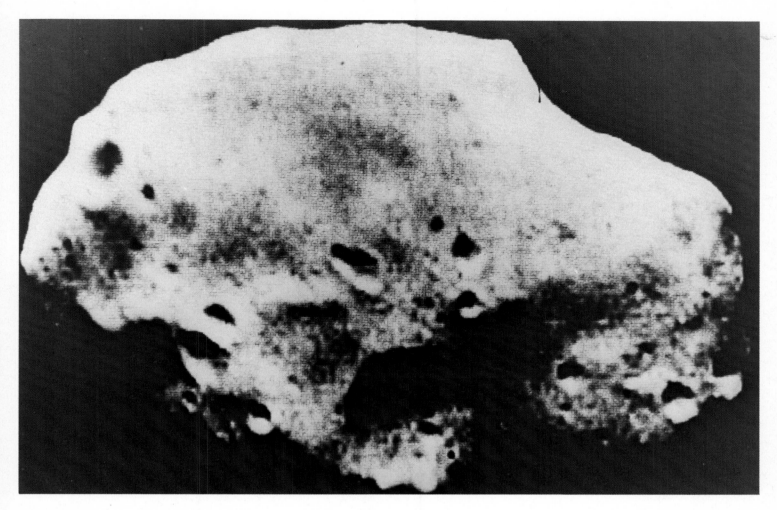

metres (20 miles), meaning that Mars must be very cold. A complete photographic survey of Mars from orbit by the American space probe Mariner 9 in 1971–72 revealed a gigantic volcano known as Olympus Mons, 600 kilometres (375 miles) wide and 24 kilometres (15 miles) high, making it the largest known volcano in the solar system – bigger even than the volcanic Hawaiian islands on Earth. Also shown was a canyon like the African rift valley, 4000 kilometres (2500 miles) long and 120 kilometres (75 miles) wide. The discovery of what appeared to be dried-up river channels on the surface increased optimism that the planet's climate may in the past have been sufficiently warm and damp for some primitive life-forms to have arisen. Two Viking spacecraft were dispatched to Mars to find out.

When the Viking landers set down on Mars in the summer of 1976, their cameras revealed a rust-red landscape with no signs of life. Fine dust particles suspended in the atmosphere turned the Martian sky pinkish-red. Measurements from the Viking landers illustrated the true harshness of the Martian environment; even on a sunny summer's afternoon the air temperature rises to only −30°C; at night, it falls to −86°C. The polar caps are made of a mixture of water ice and frozen carbon dioxide (dry ice), and there is probably a permanently frozen layer (permafrost) under all the Martian surface. Each Viking lander carried a scoop to sample the Martian surface and a miniature biological laboratory to incubate the soil in search of Martian micro-organisms. Alas, although the soil produced many interesting chemical reactions, the Vikings found no trace of even the tiniest bugs on Mars. The red planet seems to be sterile after all. Nonetheless, one day there will be life on Mars – when the first humans visit it. Such an expedition will probably not take place until around the year 2000.

Mars has two tiny moons, called Phobos and Deimos. They were discovered by the American astronomer Asaph Hall (1829–1907) during the same close approach of Mars in 1877 at which the canals were reported. Phobos, the larger of the two, is so close to Mars, 6000 kilometres (3700 miles) above the surface, that it crosses the Martian sky twice a day. Deimos is three times farther away. Space probe photographs show that Phobos and Deimos are irregularly shaped lumps of rock, probably stray bodies captured early in the history of the solar system. Their respective diameters are approximately 22 kilometres (14 miles) and 12 kilometres (8 miles).

Beyond Mars lies a belt of rubble known as the asteroids, too faint to be seen without a telescope. Ceres, the largest, 1000 kilometres (600 miles) in diameter, was discovered in 1801 by the Italian astronomer Giuseppe Piazzi (1746–1826). Now, thousands are known. Astronomers estimate that a total of 100000 asteroids may be visible in the largest telescopes, although most of these will be no more than a few hundred metres across. Typical asteroids probably resemble Phobos and Deimos. Some asteroids have eccentric orbits that take them outside the normal asteroid belt – one, called Hermes, came within 800000 kilometres (500000 miles) of the Earth in 1937 – but most orbit between Mars and Jupiter. If all the asteroids were gathered together they would make a body only one-thirtieth the mass of the Moon. They do not, therefore, represent the remains of a shattered former planet as was once suggested. Probably they are examples of the primitive bodies of the solar system from which the planets formed, but were themselves prevented from growing into anything larger by the overshadowing effect of the gravitational pull of Jupiter, the giant planet of the solar system.

Above
Jupiter seen from a distance of 2·5 million kilometres (1·58 million miles) by the Pioneer 10 space probe in December 1973, showing the red spot and the shadow of the moon Io.

Right
Saturn and its rings, as it might appear from its moon, Hyperion.

Jupiter. This planet weighs two-and-a-half times as much as all the other planets put together. It is 142 800 kilometres (88 700 miles) in diameter, eleven times that of Earth. Lying in the cold outer reaches of the solar system, 778·3 million kilometres (483·6 million miles) from the Sun, and taking 11·86 years to complete one orbit, Jupiter is different in nature from the small, rocky bodies that make up the inner solar system. It is a gas giant, composed mostly of hydrogen and helium – the same gases as the Sun. In fact, had Jupiter been about ten times bigger it would have become a small star. Since Jupiter's gravity is so great – the escape velocity is five-and-a-half times that of Earth – it has been able to retain even the lightest gases, and

so has changed little since its formation.

Through a telescope, Jupiter presents an abundance of detail. Multi-coloured cloud belts stretch around the planet, drawn out into parallel bands by Jupiter's high-speed rotation of just under 10 hours, the fastest of any planet. Traces of methane, ammonia, and other chemicals produce the colours from yellow, through red and brown, to purple and blue, seen among the continually changing spots and swirls in the Jovian clouds. The only permanent feature in Jupiter's clouds is the great red spot, an enormous oval the width of three Earths, photographed in close-up by the Pioneer 10 and 11 probes that sped past the planet in 1973 and 1974. The red spot is now believed to be a scaled-up version of the anvil-shaped clouds seen over thunderstorms on Earth, caused by a permanent updraught of hot gas from the interior of Jupiter; the spot is actually the highest cloud on Jupiter. Red phosphorus welling up from deep in the Jovian atmosphere is thought to give the spot its characteristic colour. One surprising fact

ring A

Cassini division

ring B

ring C

gap

ring D

Saturn

Right
Rings of Saturn. Saturn's rings are made of rocky particles coated with ice. There is a gap called Cassini's division between the two brightest rings, labelled A and B. Ring C, the so-called crêpe ring, is faint and transparent. Ring D, faintest of all, was discovered in 1969, apparently extending down almost to the planet's cloud tops. Some astronomers believe that a faint ring of debris may lie outside ring A.

Far right
Rings of Uranus. In 1977, astronomers discovered that Uranus has at least five rings of rocky debris. Unlike the rings of Saturn, these rings are narrow and divided by wide gaps.

confirmed by the Pioneer probes is that Jupiter releases two-and-a-half times as much heat as it receives from the Sun. This heat may be left over from its formation, or it could be released by a shrinking of the planet by an undetectable 1 millimetre (0·04 inch) per year. Whatever the cause, the internal heat stirs the continually changing cloud patterns on Jupiter.

There is probably no such things as a solid Jupiter beneath the clouds. At the cloud tops the temperature is −150°C, but lower levels of the atmosphere may be warm enough to support some kind of airborne life. About 1 000 kilometres (600 miles) below the visible cloud tops, pressures become so great that hydrogen is compressed into a liquid. Towards the planet's centre the hydrogen is squeezed even further so that it becomes electrically conducting, like a metal. Possibly Jupiter has a rocky core about the size of Mars. Convection currents in the electrically conducting hydrogen region around the core produce a strong magnetic field around Jupiter which traps atomic particles from the Sun, producing radiation belts with several hundred times the radiation dose necessary to kill a man.

Men will never be able to land on Jupiter, but they might visit several of its numerous satellites, which form a kind of mini solar system. Jupiter's thirteenth satellite was discovered in 1974, and a probable fourteenth member was reported in 1975. Ganymede and Callisto, the two largest satellites, have diameters of about 5 000 kilometres (3 100 miles), larger than the planet Mercury. Io and Europa, the other two major satellites, are similar in size to our Moon. All four, discovered by Galileo, can be seen with binoculars.

Saturn. This is perhaps the most beautiful planet of all, the outermost planet visible with the naked eye, 1 427 million kilometres (887 million miles) from the Sun and taking 29·5 years to complete one orbit. Saturn, another gas giant composed mostly of hydrogen and helium, is noted for the rings which encircle its equator. These rings are made of rocky particles about the size of bricks, coated with frozen water, orbiting Saturn like a swarm of moonlets. From rim to rim the rings stretch for 275 000 kilometres (170 000 miles), yet they are less than 16 kilometres (10 miles) thick from top to bottom. Therefore, in relation to their diameter, they are thinner than a sheet of

paper. Either the rings were produced when a former moon of Saturn strayed too close to the planet and was broken up by the strong gravitational force, or they could represent the building blocks of a potential moon that never formed. Small telescopes will show the rings; in larger telescopes the bright outer part of the ring is seen to be separated from the dimmer inner part by a 2 700-kilometre (1 700-mile) gap, named Cassini's division after the French astronomer Jean Dominique Cassini (1625–1712) who detected it in 1675. On the inner side of these rings is the transparent crêpe ring. In 1969, a faint, innermost, fourth ring was detected, extending down to the cloud tops of Saturn.

Saturn is the second largest planet in the solar system, 120 000 kilometres (74 500 miles) in diameter, and its rotation period, 10·25 hours, is second only to that of Jupiter. Saturn's cloud belts are less distinct and less turbulent than those of Jupiter, and there is no equivalent of the red spot. Although Saturn is similar in composition to Jupiter, the gases of which it is made are not compressed so tightly, so its overall density is much less. In fact, Saturn

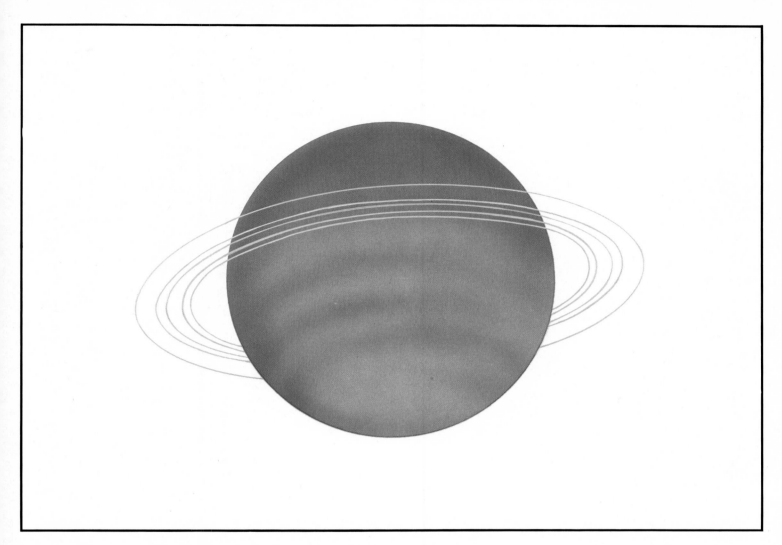

is less dense than water; given a big enough ocean, Saturn would float.

Among Saturn's ten satellites is Titan, the only moon in the solar system known to possess a substantial atmosphere. Dense clouds of methane and other gases surround Titan. Its diameter of about 5 800 kilometres (3 600 miles) is greater than that of any of Jupiter's moons; only Neptune's biggest moon, Triton, may be larger. Close-up views of Saturn should be obtained in 1979 when the Pioneer 11 space probe reaches the planet. Voyager 1 and 2, launched in the summer of 1977, will be looking at Jupiter and Saturn in even more detail in 1979 and 1981 respectively.

Uranus. In 1781, Sir William Herschel doubled the known size of the solar system when he discovered the planet Uranus, 2 870 million kilometres (1 783 million miles) from the Sun, twice as far as Saturn. Uranus is remarkable in that it seems to have fallen on its side; its axis of rotation lies almost exactly in the plane of its orbit, so that each pole is subjected to 42 years of perpetual sunlight, followed by 42 years of perpetual darkness, as the planet completes its 84-year orbit around the Sun. No-one knows the reason

for this exaggerated tilt, but it must have come about during the planet's formation, perhaps as the result of a collision.

Uranus appears greenish because, among the hydrogen and helium of its atmosphere, there are considerable amounts of methane, which absorbs red light. (Methane is the so-called 'natural gas' we burn in cookers on Earth.) Beneath the featureless green clouds, over half the 51 800-kilometre (32 200-mile) diameter of Uranus is made up of a core of rock and ice, mostly frozen water and ammonia. The planet's rotation rate is still uncertain; in the 1920s it was estimated that Uranus spins once every 11 hours, but recent measurements suggest that its rotation rate is actually twice as long, 22 hours.

Uranus has five known moons, all of which orbit around its equator; therefore, they, too, are highly inclined to the plane of the planet's orbit. Between 18 000 and 25 000 kilometres (11 200–15 500 miles) from the cloud tops lie five thin rings of rocky debris, discovered in 1977. They are too faint to be seen directly, but were discovered when they blocked out light from a star that Uranus passed in front of. The four innermost rings are 10 kilo-

metres (6 miles) wide, while the outermost ring has a width of 100 kilometres (60 miles). As with the rings of Saturn, they are either the remnants of a shattered former moon, or they are pieces that were never collected up into a satellite. If all goes well, one of the two Voyager spacecraft sent to study Jupiter and Saturn will be sent on to look at Uranus, arriving there by 1986.

Neptune. After Herschel's discovery of Uranus, astronomers found that the planet was not keeping to its predicted path. Something seemed to be pulling it out of line – perhaps another as yet undiscovered planet. Mathematicians started to calculate the possible position of this planet. In England, John Couch Adams (1819–1892), and in France, Urbain Leverrier (1811–1877), reached almost identical conclusions, and on September 23, 1846, the German astronomer Johann Gottfried Galle (1812–1910) found the new planet close to the predicted position. It was named Neptune.

Neptune orbits the Sun every 165 years at an average distance of 4 500 million kilometres (2 800 million miles). Like Uranus it appears as a green, featureless disc in a telescope, and in fact the two planets are

Neptune as it might appear from one of its moons, Triton.

believed to be almost identical in composition and structure. Neptune is slightly the smaller of the two, being 49 500 kilometres (30 800 miles) in diameter. Old measurements of its rotation give a period of 16 hours but, as with Uranus, this is open to considerable revision by newer results. Neptune has two satellites, both extraordinary: Triton, estimated to be 6 000 kilometres (3 700 miles) in diameter, may be the largest moon in the solar system. It orbits Neptune from east to west, the reverse of the normal west-to-east traffic pattern in the solar system. Nereid, the more distant moon, moves in the standard west-to-east direction, but its orbit is the most elongated of any moon, ranging between 1·3 million and 9·8 million kilometres (0·83 – 6·1 million miles) from the planet.

Pluto. After the discovery of Neptune it was natural that astronomers should go hunting for other possible planets. Most dedicated was Percival Lowell (an advocate of the Martian canal theory), who instituted a photographic search for a trans-Neptunian planet at his observatory in Arizona. Not until long after Lowell's death did the search produce results, when Clyde Tombaugh (b. 1906) discovered tiny Pluto on February 18, 1930. Pluto is so slow-moving that it takes 248 years to complete one orbit of the Sun, and so will not return to its discovery position until 2178. Pluto's diameter is difficult to measure properly, but it is certainly small, under 6 000 kilometres (3 600 miles). Recent observations suggest it may be only about 3 000 kilometres in diameter, less than our own Moon, and therefore the smallest planet of all. Part of its surface is covered with frozen methane, at a temperature of −230°C. From Pluto, the Sun appears as nothing more than a bright star. One figure that does seem well

established is the planet's rotation period, 6 days 9 hours.

Pluto's average distance from the Sun is 5 900 million kilometres (3 600 million miles), but its orbit is actually quite eccentric and at its closest it can come within the orbit of Neptune. In fact it does so between January 1979 and March 1999; during that time, Neptune will be the outermost planet of the solar system. Pluto is the only planet to cross another's orbit. This erratic behaviour, combined with its small size, suggests that Pluto may actually be an escaped satellite of Neptune, ejected in a near-collision that threw the other two satellites into their peculiar orbits. Pluto has no moons of its own.

Comets. Are there other planets beyond Pluto? Probably not. Any other planets would have to be either extremely small, or extremely distant, or both, to have escaped detection by now. Beyond Pluto

there is probably nothing more than a belt of millions upon millions of comets, the ghostly wanderers of the solar system which loop around the Sun on highly extended orbits lasting up to millions of years. At their farthest, comets can travel halfway to the nearest star, but still be held by the Sun's gravity. Comets can be trapped by the gravitational pulls of the planets into much shorter orbits, such as Comet Encke which has the shortest known period, 3·3 years.

Far from the Sun, a comet is believed to resemble a dirty snowball – a bag of rocks and dust cemented into a ball a few kilometres across by frozen gas. As a comet plunges in towards the Sun it warms up and the gases evaporate to form a glowing head perhaps 100 000 kilometres (62 000 miles) across and a long, flowing tail which in the case of Halley's comet in 1910 stretched for 150 million kilometres (93 million miles), as far as from the Earth to the

From Pluto, the outermost planet of our solar system, the Sun appears as a bright star.

ISTI MIRANT STELLA

HAROLD

Sun. Halley's comet, which orbits the Sun every 76 years, is due back in 1986. Named after the English astronomer Edmond Halley (1656–1742), who calculated its orbit in 1705, it moves from between the orbits of Mercury and Venus out to beyond the orbit of Neptune, and is believed to have been first seen in 466 BC. Despite their apparent grandeur, comets are so insubstantial that it would take a million million of them to outweigh the Earth.

Meteors and meteorites. Comets lose gas and dust each time they approach the Sun, and eventually fade out. Dust particles from comets are being swept up by the Earth all the time; they burn up in the atmosphere by friction to form the darting streaks of light known as shooting stars or meteors. Meteors are about

the size of grains of sand, too small to reach the ground. Occasionally, much larger chunks of rock and metal, known as meteorites, penetrate the atmosphere, which do not come from comets but instead are probably fragments of asteroids. At Hoba West in Namibia (South West Africa) lies the heaviest known meteorite, a chunk of iron and nickel weighing 70 tonnes. If a meteorite hits the Earth at a high enough speed it will blast out a crater like those on the Moon. A giant crater over 1 kilometre across in the Arizona desert was formed about 50 000 years ago by the impact of an iron meteorite weighing a quarter of a million tonnes, which exploded with sufficient force to devastate a city. Fortunately, encounters with such bodies are rare.

Opposite above
Meteor crater near Winslow, Arizona, 1 kilometre (0·62 mile) in diameter, was blasted out by the impact of a giant meteorite 50 000 years or so ago.

Opposite below
Halley's comet, shown on the Bayeux tapestry.

Above
Comet Ikeya-Seki rising in the morning sky on October 28, 1965, near Los Alamos, New Mexico.

The Sun and other stars

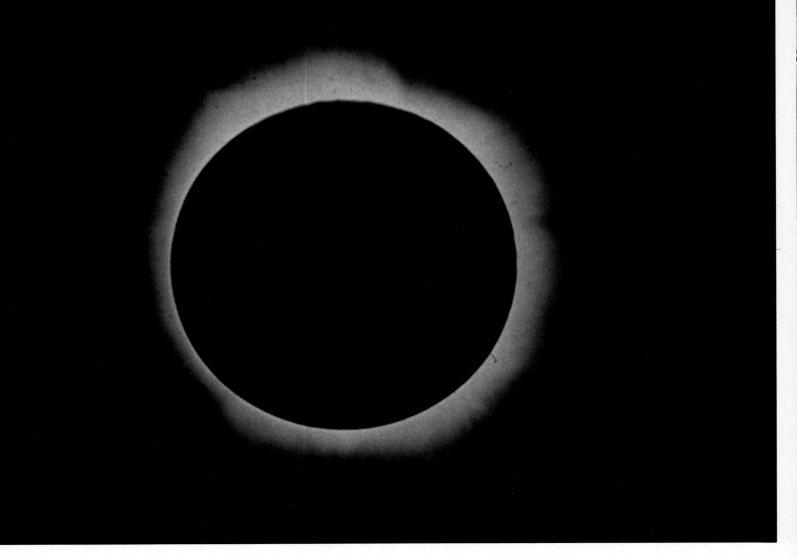

Total eclipse of the Sun, showing the inner part of the Sun's pearly corona.

Life on Earth would be impossible without the Sun, our prime energy source. The Sun's heat keeps temperatures on Earth warm enough for life, and its light is used by plants for energy to grow. When we burn fossil fuels – coal, oil and natural gas – we are actually releasing the stored energy of sunlight. In the future we shall be able to harness sunlight directly to provide many of our energy needs.

The Sun is a glowing ball of gas of awesome size – its diameter of 1 392 000 kilometres (865 000 miles) is equivalent to a row of 109 Earths. At our distance of 149 600 000 kilometres (93 million miles) the Sun appears comfortably warm and bright. If we were closer to the Sun, at the distance of Mercury or Venus, conditions would be too hot for life, whereas farther away, at the orbit of Mars or beyond, sunlight would be too weak.

From our uniquely favourable position in orbit around the Sun we can observe its surface in some detail. One important point to bear in mind is that you should *never* look directly at the Sun through any form of optical instrument; even staring at the Sun for long periods can be dangerous. The only safe way to study the Sun is to clamp the telescope or binoculars firmly in position and project the Sun's image on to a piece of white card. The penalty for attempting to view the Sun directly is blindness.

As astronomers turned their telescopes on the Sun in the seventeenth century, they saw that its surface was frequently blemished by variable dark patches, known as sunspots. Most spots are at least the size of the Earth, and some large groups stretch for 150 000 kilometres (93 000 miles) or more – half the distance from the Earth to the Moon. An average spot lasts for a week, although some have been followed for months. By observing the passage of these spots across the Sun's face, astronomers found that the Sun's speed of rotation varied from once every 25 days at the equator to 34 days towards the poles. The fact that the Sun did not rotate uniformly showed that it could not be a solid body, but must be composed of incandescent gas.

In 1843, the German astronomer, Heinrich Schwabe (1789–1875), found after years of observation that the number of sunspots waxes and wanes in a cycle that is now estimated to last approximately 11 years. At maximum there may be dozens of sunspots visible at a time, whereas at minimum there may be no sunspots seen for days on end. The last sunspot minimum occurred in 1976; the next maximum is predicted for 1982. The overall storminess of the Sun's surface also varies in this same cycle, including eruptions known as flares that fling out atomic particles into space and produce radio blackouts on Earth. Actually, in each successive sunspot cycle the north and south magnetic poles of the Sun are reversed, so that a complete solar cycle is now taken to last 22 years.

Weather patterns on Earth, including rainfall and temperature, seem to change with the sunspot cycle. Astronomers, looking back through old records, have found that the solar cycle can be very erratic; from 1640 to 1720 almost no sunspots were seen, and this period coincided with a time of abnormally low temperatures known as the Little Ice Age. Fortunately, we now seem to be in a period of high solar activity and relatively warm temperatures. Why the Sun should have such a variable pulse of activity, and how it affects the climate on Earth, is unknown.

What makes the Sun shine? If it were burning like a lump of coal, it would become a dull, burnt-out ember in only a few thousand years. A century ago it was assumed that the Sun produced its energy by slowly contracting at the undetectable rate of a kilometre or two every 10 years; such a gradual process would release enough heat to keep the Sun shining for perhaps 100 million years. However, geologists subsequently found that the rocks of Earth are thousands of millions of years old; the most recent evidence from the dating of Earth rocks, Moon rocks, and meteorites has shown that the entire solar system is 4 600 million years old. To explain what kept the Sun alight for up to 100 times longer than could be explained by contraction, an entirely new source of power was needed.

The answer came earlier this century with the discovery of the energy contained within the nucleus of the atom. In 1938, the physicist Hans Bethe (b. 1906) showed that the centre of the Sun is a nuclear powerhouse, turning hydrogen into helium by a series of nuclear reactions, and releasing energy as it does so.

Analysis of light from the Sun shows that it is composed of about 70 per cent hydrogen, the lightest and simplest substance in the universe, with most of the rest consisting of helium, the second simplest substance. All the other known

Hot gas swirls along lines of magnetic force near a dark sunspot.

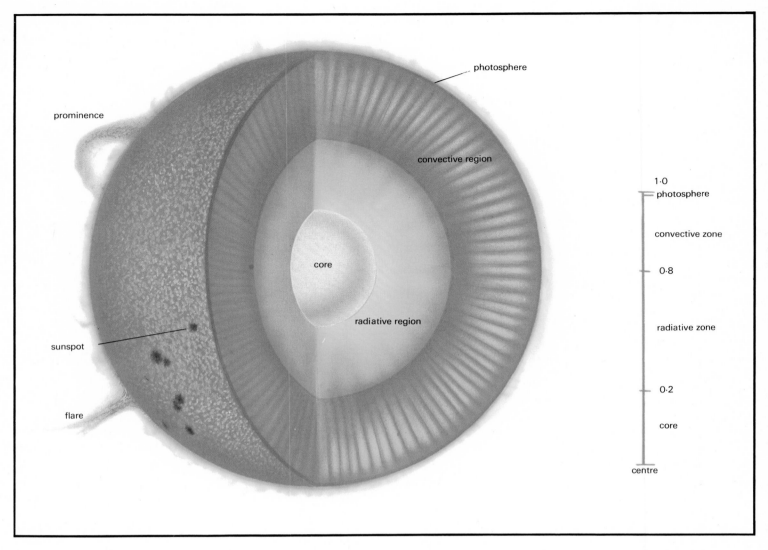

prominence

photosphere

convective region

core

radiative region

sunspot

flare

1·0
photosphere

convective zone

0·8

radiative zone

0·2

core

centre

Cutaway of the Sun, showing the various layers. Energy is generated by nuclear reactions at the Sun's core. The energy travels about four-fifths of the way to the surface in the form of radiation, but completes the journey in the form of giant convection cells of gas.

chemical elements make up only one or two per cent of the Sun. At the centre of the Sun, where temperatures must reach 15 million °C and matter is packed 100 times as densely as water, fusion reactions take place like those in a hydrogen bomb. In the reactions, four hydrogen nuclei are fused together to form one helium nucleus. But a helium nucleus is fractionally lighter than four hydrogen nuclei; where does the 'missing mass' go? The answer is that it is turned into energy, and it is this energy that powers the Sun. Albert Einstein showed in his theory of relativity that matter can be converted into energy, and here in the Sun is the proof. Every second, 600 million tonnes of hydrogen are turned into helium inside the Sun, with 4 million tonnes of hydrogen being converted into energy in the process. The Sun is so massive that, even generating energy at this prodigious rate, it can live for a total of 10 000 million years. It is approximately halfway through its life at present.

Fortunately for us, this fusion reaction proceeds smoothly so the Sun does not fly apart in a bomb-burst. The energy created travels in the form of high-energy radiation, such as X-rays, for most of the way towards the surface but completes the journey in gigantic circulating convection cells of hot gas. At the visible surface of the Sun, called the *photosphere*, the temperature has dropped to 6 000°C.

The photosphere (its name means 'sphere of light') is a layer about 300 kilometres (200 miles) thick, and although it looks solid it is actually made of gas 10 000 times less dense than the Earth's atmosphere. Convection cells of gas about 1 000 kilometres (600 miles) across bubble up through the photosphere like water boiling in a pan, giving a characteristic 'rice-grain' effect to the photosphere. It is on the photosphere that sunspots occur. They are areas of cooler gas, about 4 500°C, that appear dark by contrast with the more brilliant surrounding layers. Sunspots are believed to be caused by magnetic fields bursting through the surface of the Sun and blocking the outward flow of heat.

Above the photosphere is a layer of gas about 16 000 kilometres (10 000 miles) deep known as the *chromosphere*, meaning colour sphere. It is visible only at total solar eclipses

Comparison of sizes and colours of various stars, from red and blue giants to red and white dwarfs.

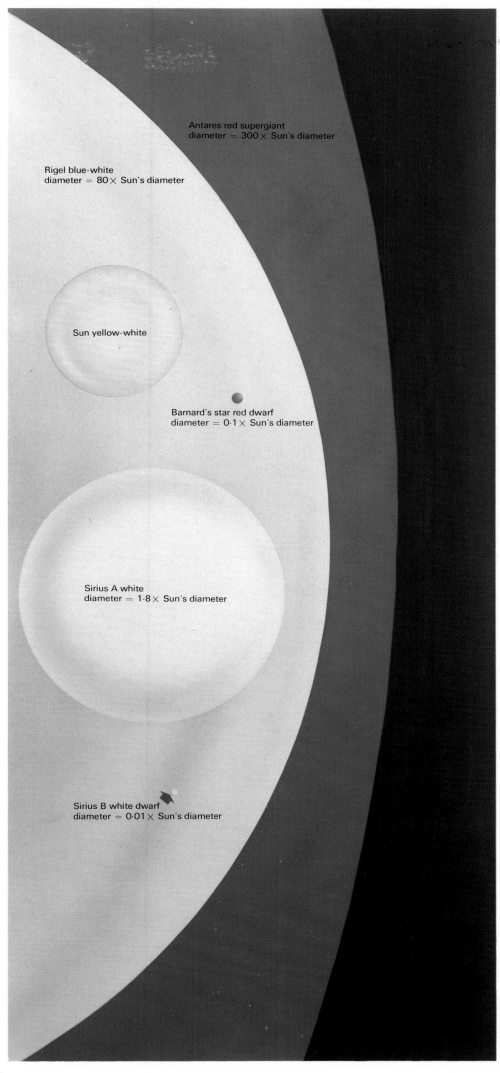

Antares red supergiant
diameter = 300 × Sun's diameter

Rigel blue-white
diameter = 80 × Sun's diameter

Sun yellow-white

Barnard's star red dwarf
diameter = 0·1 × Sun's diameter

Sirius A white
diameter = 1·8 × Sun's diameter

Sirius B white dwarf
diameter = 0·01 × Sun's diameter

when the disc of the Moon blocks light from the far more brilliant photosphere. The chromosphere gets its name from its beautiful pinkish-red colour, caused by glowing hydrogen gas. Jets of hot gas known as spicules jut up through the chromosphere, giving its upper edge a jagged appearance.

Also visible from time to time at the edge of the Sun are glowing loops of gas known as prominences. Some prominences stretch away from the Sun's surface like giant arches, thousands of kilometres long, and can last for weeks or months; these so-called quiescent prominences are associated with the magnetic fields that loop out of the Sun's surface like strands from a tangled ball of yarn. Other types, known as surge prominences, eject material at up to 1 000 kilometres (600 miles) per second from flares on the photosphere. The atomic particles ejected in this way reach the Earth, where they cause radio interference and produce the glowing atmospheric effects known as aurorae. All these effects wax and wane with the sunspot cycle.

The outermost layer around the Sun is the *corona*, visible as a faint, pearly coloured halo of light during a total eclipse. The corona is composed of hot gas boiled off from the Sun and streaming outwards into space to form what is known as the solar wind. Atomic particles of the solar wind are detected flowing past the Earth; therefore, it can be said that we are in the outermost regions of the Sun's corona.

Stars come in many sizes and brightnesses. Some are much bigger and brighter than the Sun, while others are smaller and fainter. For instance, the red supergiant star Betelgeuse is 300 to 400 times the diameter of the Sun and gives out 15 000 times as much light. The red dwarf Barnard's star is only about one-tenth the Sun's diameter and gives out one two-thousandth of the Sun's light, so that it cannot be seen without a telescope.

Although all stars at first glance appear white, closer inspection shows that they are different colours, which are a guide to their surface temperatures. The hottest stars appear blue or white, whereas the coolest ones appear orange or red. The Sun, which is yellow, is average both in

Left
A prominence, an eruption on the Sun's
surface in which clouds of hot gas are
ejected hundreds of thousands of kilometres into space, photographed by the
Skylab astronauts.

Right
Stars in a constellation may all be at
widely differing distances from Earth.
Shown here is the famous W-shaped
constellation of Cassiopeia as it is seen
from Earth, with the actual positions of
the stars indicated at the ends of the
dotted lines.

Below
Cepheid variable stars swell and contract
in a regular way, changing in brightness
as they do so. The time a Cepheid variable
takes to complete a cycle is the key to its
average brightness, which serves as a vital
distance indicator to astronomers.

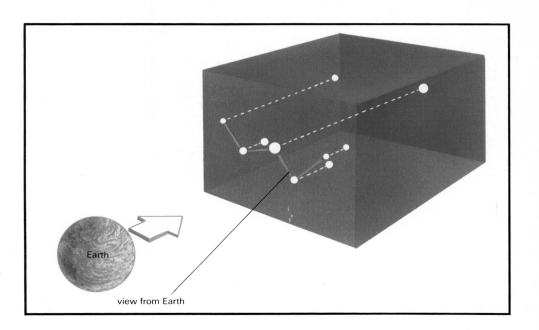

view from Earth

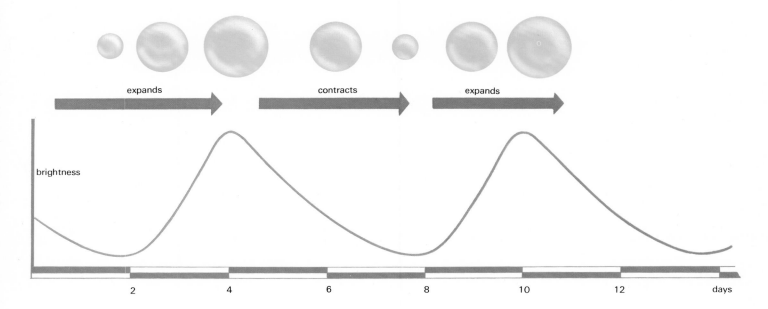

expands → contracts → expands

brightness

2   4   6   8   10   12   days

size and temperature. Analysis of a
star's light reveals whether it is a hot
giant star or a cool dwarf, so that
astronomers can calculate how luminous it is.

However the distances of the
stars also affect how bright they
appear to us. Astronomers express
stellar distances in terms of light
years, the distance that light, travelling at 300 000 kilometres (186 000
miles) per second, would cover in a
year; a light year is equivalent to 9·5
million million kilometres (6 million
million miles). If our Sun were taken
to the position of the nearest star,
Alpha Centauri, 4·3 light years away,
it would appear as an averagely
bright night-sky star. At a distance of
50 light years or so, the Sun would be
too faint to see without a telescope.
Sirius appears the brightest star in the
sky simply because it is relatively
close, 8·7 light years away. The star
Deneb, in Cygnus, gives out 2 000
times as much light as Sirius but it

appears fainter to us because it is
200 times farther away. By compar-
ing the calculated value of a star's
luminosity with how bright it actually appears in the sky, astronomers
can estimate the star's distance.

An important application of this
principle is provided by stars that
have a built-in brightness indicator
which is far more accurate than that
obtainable by analysis of their light.
These are known as Cepheid variable
stars, after their prototype, Delta
Cephei. Cepheid variables change in
brightness every few days as they
expand and contract in size, like a
slowly beating heart. A Cepheid
variable's heartbeat is directly related
to its intrinsic brightness, so that by
measuring the period of such a
heartbeat, astronomers can work out
exactly how bright it ought to
appear. The difference between this
so-called *absolute magnitude* and the
brightness as observed in the sky (the
apparent magnitude) reveals the star's

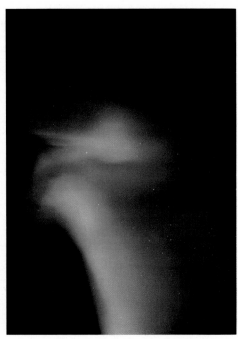

The aurora borealis, commonly termed
the northern lights, is an electric glow in
the Earth's upper atmosphere caused by
atomic particles ejected from outbursts on
the Sun.

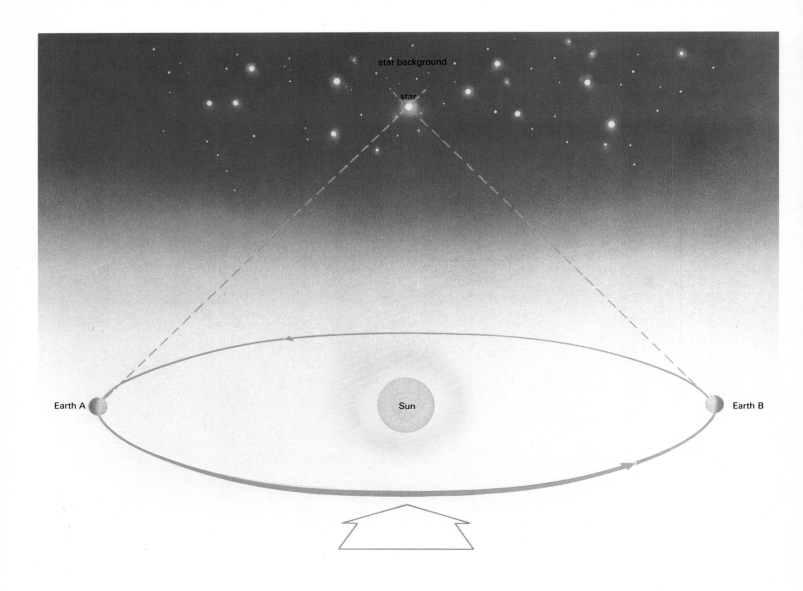

star background

star

Earth A

Sun

Earth B

distance. This technique produces much more accurate distance measurements than the method of analysing the star's light described above, but it is hampered by the fact that Cepheid variables are relatively rare stars – less than 1 000 are known in our galaxy. Nonetheless, Cepheid variables have proved vital distance indicators in astronomy.

The only direct way of measuring a star's distance is by *parallax*, or its shift in position as seen from opposite sides of the Earth's orbit. This technique relies on nothing more than simple trigonometry, as in measuring the distance of a tree or church tower by reference to background objects as seen from two different positions. A star's position is measured relative to background stars, and then is re-measured six months later when the Earth has moved around to the other side of its orbit. The amount of shift reveals the star's distance, the nearest stars showing the greatest parallax. The German astronomer, Friedrich Bessel (1784–1846), in 1838 first

measured the parallax of a star, 61 Cygni. Bessel calculated that 61 Cygni lay 10 light years away; modern measurements have refined the distance to 11·2 light years, but even so 61 Cygni is still among the twenty nearest stars. Unfortunately, beyond about 100 light years the parallax shift becomes too small to be measured accurately, and astronomers have to rely on the indirect methods of brightness comparisons described above.

Many stars other than Cepheids vary in brightness. In 1975 a total of over 25 000 variable stars were listed and more are being discovered all the time. Some of them vary regularly, like the Cepheids, but others are much more erratic, notably red giants and supergiants such as Betelgeuse, 650 light years away, which are so distended that they become unstable and vary irregularly in size and brightness. Amateur astronomers make important contributions by monitoring the light changes of these stars.

Above
Distances of the nearest stars can be measured by plotting their change in position (parallax) against more distant stars as seen from opposite sides of the Earth's orbit (positions A and B). The amount of parallax depends on the star's distance from Earth, being greatest for the nearest stars.

Above right
How a stellar explosion, or nova, occurs. Two stars, one ordinary, one a white dwarf, orbit each other (a). Gas flows from the surface of the ordinary star on to the white dwarf (b), where it ignites in a nuclear explosion and an expanding shell of gas is thrown off (c).

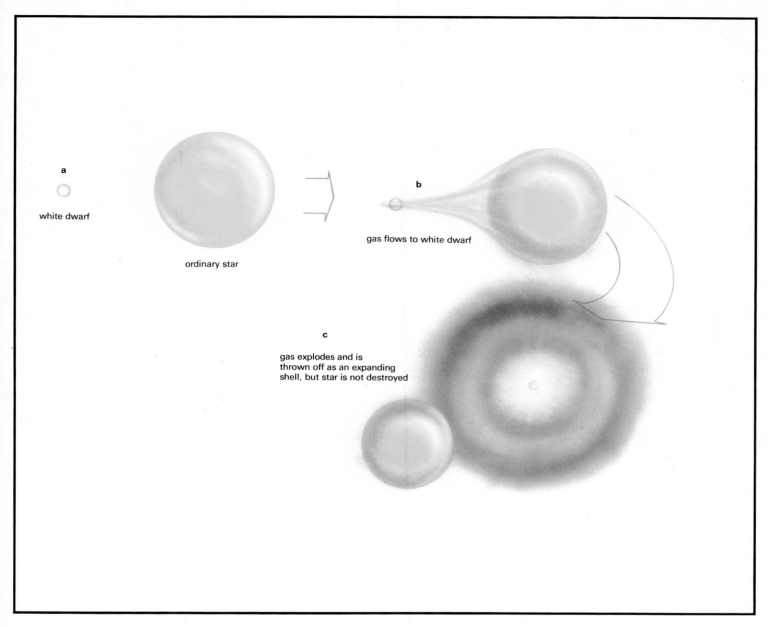

a
white dwarf

ordinary star

b
gas flows to white dwarf

c
gas explodes and is
thrown off as an expanding
shell, but star is not destroyed

Other variables involve systems in which matter flows between two stars close together, causing sudden eruptions of light. The most spectacular examples of such variables are the novae, a name which comes from the Latin word meaning new. They flare up in the sky where no bright star was seen before, and ancient astronomers believed they really were new stars. Actually, what has happened is that a formerly faint star has increased by 10 000 times or more in brightness. A nova rises to maximum brightness in a day or two before sinking back into obscurity over days, months, or sometimes years. Novae are believed to be double star systems in which a white dwarf orbits with another star. Gas from the outer regions of the other star falls on the white dwarf, ignites, and is thrown off, causing the sudden surge in brightness. This process can happen more than once, and several novae have been seen to recur after intervals of a few years. Amateur astronomers are often the first to

spot and report these unexpected stellar eruptions. In a nova explosion only a thin shell of gas is thrown off; the star itself does not blow up. By contrast, supernovae are the even more brilliant detonations of massive stars, which blow themselves to pieces at the ends of their lives. Supernovae are much less common than novae, and none have been seen in our galaxy since 1604.

Most stars are not single like the Sun, but come in twos, threes, or larger groups. The bright star Castor in the constellation Gemini, for example, is actually a system of six close stars, although only one is visible to the naked eye. A widely spaced double star is the second star along the handle of the Plough, known as Mizar. Looking closely, you will see a fainter star near Mizar; this companion star is called Alcor. A telescope reveals an even fainter star between Mizar and Alcor. Analysis of the spectrum of light from Alcor and this fainter star shows that they both have stars orbiting them,

too close to be seen separately; they are known as *spectroscopic binaries*. All five stars of the Mizar-Alcor system, 88 light years away, are linked by gravity. Alpha Centauri, the closest star to the Sun, is a system of three stars. Binoculars or a telescope reveal that Alpha Centauri itself, which to the naked eye appears as a single brilliant star, is actually double. The third star is a faint red dwarf, called Proxima Centauri because it lies fractionally closer to us than the other two stars. All three stars of Alpha Centauri lie approximately 4·3 light years away.

When one member of a close double star system moves in front of its companion, the star's total light as seen from Earth drops temporarily. This is known as an eclipsing binary star. A famous example is the star Algol in the constellation Perseus, which drops in brightness every 2·87 days as it is eclipsed by a fainter companion star. The brightness changes of Algol were first explained in 1783 by the English amateur

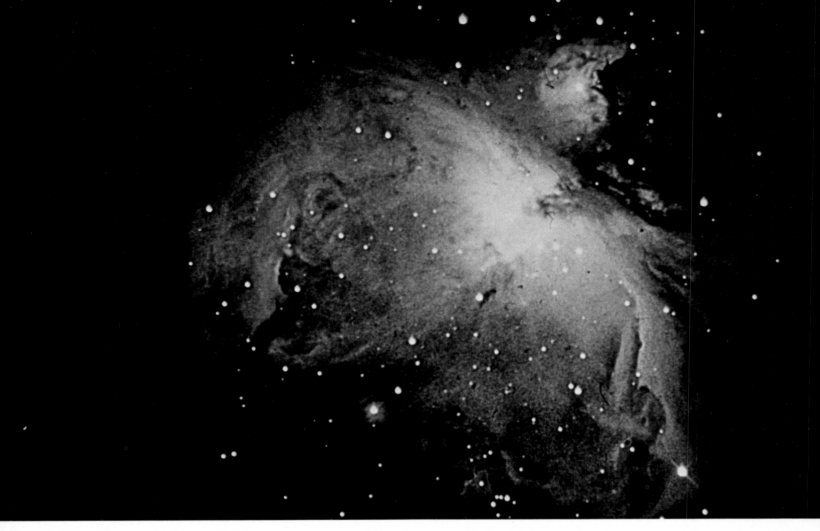

Orion nebula, M42, a glowing cloud of gas, is a birthplace of stars. It is illuminated by light from new-born stars at its centre.

Algol is an eclipsing binary, in which two stars periodically eclipse each other, as seen from Earth, causing the total brightness of Algol to vary. The bigger of the two stars is actually the fainter, so that its eclipses produce a smaller drop in light than when the smaller and brighter star is eclipsed.

astronomer John Goodricke (1764–1786) from his own naked-eye observations of the star's light changes. Goodricke, in 1784, discovered another notable eclipsing binary star, Beta Lyrae, which varies in brightness every 12·9 days. These two stars are so close that they are distorted into egg shapes by each other's gravity. Hot gas from the surface of the stars is spiralling away into space.

Stars are born from vast clouds of gas and dust known as *nebulae*, the Latin for cloud. Nebulae are plentiful throughout the galaxy. One famous example is the Orion nebula, visible to the naked eye as a fuzzy patch making up part of Orion's

sword. Four new-born stars lie at the heart of the Orion nebula, and it is the light from the brightest of these that makes the nebula shine. Radio astronomers have detected an even larger dark cloud behind the visible bright region of the Orion nebula. Within this dark region are stars that have not yet 'switched on'. The Orion nebula, about 15 light years in diameter, is estimated to contain enough material to make a cluster of hundreds of stars. Long-exposure photographs through large telescopes reveal other giant clouds which are spawning groups of stars.

Stars begin to form as a cloud breaks up into smaller, denser blobs

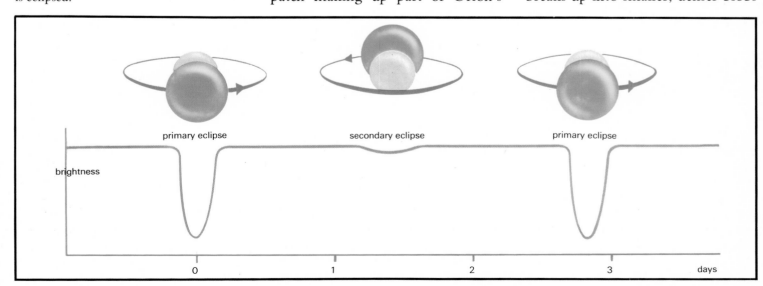

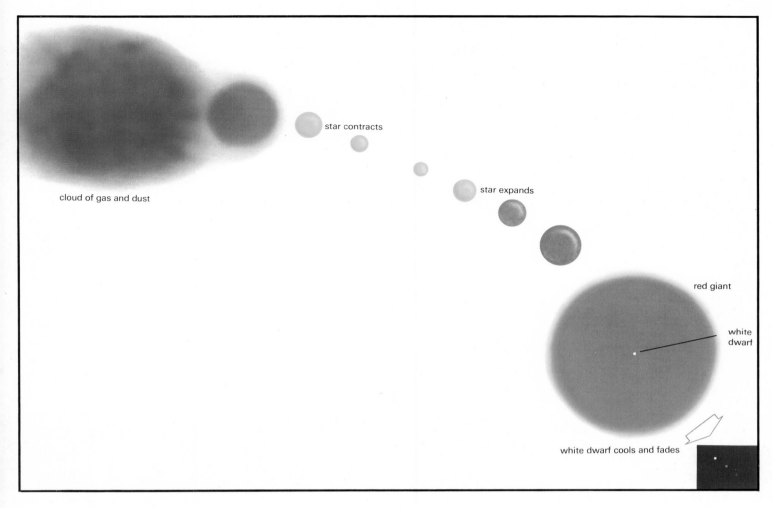

cloud of gas and dust

star contracts

star expands

red giant

white dwarf

white dwarf cools and fades

known as globules; some globules can be seen silhouetted against the brightly glowing background of certain nebulae. A typical globule is about the size of the solar system, and contains enough mass to make a star the size of the Sun. As the globule shrinks under the inward pull of its own gravity it heats up and begins to glow feebly; it has become a *protostar*. Eventually, perhaps 10 million years or so after the beginning of contraction in the case of our Sun, pressures and temperatures at the protostar's heart have risen sufficiently for nuclear reactions to begin. A star has been born.

If a globule is spinning too fast it will break up as it contracts, thereby producing a close double star. Globules that arise close together may remain bound by their mutual gravitational attraction, giving rise to double or multiple stars. Not all of the material from the globule may go into the star. Some of it may remain orbiting the star in a disc, from which a planetary system may form, as described in the previous chapter. Astronomers estimate that one star in ten may have planets.

Calculations by theorists show that for a globule with mass less than one-tenth that of the Sun, conditions at the centre never become extreme enough for nuclear reactions to

begin, and so the object never becomes a true star. Stars just above this mass limit are known as red dwarfs; they may be the most abundant stars in the sky. Proxima Centauri is a red dwarf, as is Barnard's star, the second closest star to the Sun, 6 light years away. Despite their closeness to us, these two stars are so dim that they are invisible without a telescope. Red dwarfs burn their hydrogen fuel so slowly that, despite their small size, they can live far longer than the Sun, up to a million million years.

Theorists believe that stars cannot exist with a mass greater than about 60 Suns, because they would be unstable and break up. A double star in the constellation Monoceros, known as Plaskett's star after the Canadian astronomer J. S. Plaskett who first studied it in 1922, consists of two stars each of about 60 solar masses, making it the most massive pair known.

When a large nebula fragments into stars it forms a cluster, such as the group known as the Pleiades in the constellation Taurus. Six or seven of the Pleiades are visible to the naked eye (hence the group's popular name, the Seven Sisters). The youngest members of the Pleiades are no more than one or two million years old; long-exposure photo-

The life of a star like the Sun. Stars are born from vast clouds of gas and dust in space. As the young star shrinks under the inward pull of its own gravity, it starts to heat up. Eventually, nuclear reactions turn on at its centre which power it for the rest of its life. Once it starts to run out of nuclear fuel at its centre, the star begins to swell up into a red giant, puffing off its outer layers into space to form a planetary nebula, leaving its hot core as a tiny white dwarf which slowly cools and fades.

graphs show that they are still surrounded by remnants of the cloud from which they were formed. When the Sun was born, 4 600 million years ago, it was probably a member of a cluster. Over hundreds of millions of years the members of the cluster drifted apart, as will eventually happen to the Pleiades.

Nebulae are composed mostly of hydrogen and helium gas, so that this is also the composition of stars. The burning of hydrogen into helium by nuclear reactions powers a star for the main part of its life. The Sun is in stable middle age, about halfway through this hydrogen-burning stage. There is certainly no worry that the Sun will radically change its output for thousands of millions of years yet.

Eventually a star begins to run out of hydrogen at its centre, having turned it all into helium. In search of new hydrogen fuel, the nuclear reactions move outwards into the region around the star's core. Here, with more hydrogen to burn, the reactions produce more energy. At the same time, the star's helium core begins to contract, heating up as it does so until it becomes hot enough for the helium nuclei to enter into nuclear reactions of their own, being fused together to form carbon.

With all this extra energy being released at its centre, the star swells up in size. Although the core of the star is getting hotter, as the outer layers expand they turn cooler and redder. The star therefore becomes a red giant, like the star Aldebaran which forms the glinting red eye of Taurus, the bull. Our Sun will enter this stage about 5 000 million years from now. It will swell to about 100 times its present size, engulfing the planets Mercury, Venus, and perhaps even the Earth. All life will have been extinguished on our planet long before this happens, of course. Once the Sun starts to heat up, temperatures on Earth will rise, causing widespread changes in climate, the melting of the polar caps and consequent flooding of lowland areas. Soon, it will become too hot for any form of life. The seas will evaporate, leaving a parched and barren wilderness. As the Sun swells further, shining 1 000 times as brightly as today, the Earth will be roasted to a cinder in space. Our world will indeed end in fire.

After its brief excursion into superstardom, our Sun is doomed. When the Sun reaches its maximum size, its distended outer layers become unstable. They gently drift off into space, forming a transparent shell of gas like the ring nebula in Lyra, which resembles a giant smoke ring in space. Such nebulae are called planetary nebulae, not because they have anything to do with planets, but be-

cause in small telescopes they show a planet-like disc.

At the centre of a planetary nebula lies the tiny, hot core of the former red giant. This is known as a white dwarf star. A white dwarf can contain perhaps a quarter of the star's original mass, packed into a ball no bigger than the Earth. White dwarfs are so dense that a thimbleful of material from one would weigh 10

Below left
Pleiades star cluster in Taurus is a group of about 200 stars born in the past 50 million years, and still surrounded by some of the material from which they were born.

At the end of its life, a star like the Sun swells into a red giant and then puffs off its outer layers to form a celestial smoke ring known as a planetary nebula, like NGC 6781 in Aquila (*below*), and the famous ring nebula, M 57, in Lyra (*right*). At the centre of these nebulae, the star's hot core is left as a white dwarf.

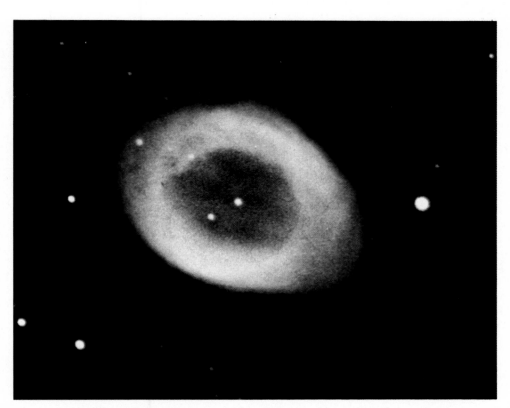

tonnes. Because they are so small,
white dwarfs give out only a fraction
of the Sun's heat and light. Sirius, the
brightest star in the sky, has a white
dwarf companion, too faint to be
seen without a telescope. This is the
remains of a former companion star
that evolved more quickly. White
dwarfs are bankrupt stars, with no
more nuclear reactions going on at
their cores to produce energy. Over
thousands of millions of years a white
dwarf cools to a dead ember in space.
Thus our once-proud Sun will end
its life as a cold, dark, and invisible
ball.

How quickly a star evolves depends on its mass. As we have said,
red dwarf stars age much more
slowly than our own Sun. By contrast, the largest stars burn out the
quickest. If the Sun had 25 per cent
more mass, it would already have
burned out. Sirius, which is over
twice as massive as the Sun, can live
for no more than about 1 000 million
years, one tenth that of the Sun. A
star with ten times the Sun's mass
burns out in one hundredth of the
Sun's lifetime. The largest known
stars, such as the two components of
Plaskett's star, live for no more than
a few million years.

The early evolution of massive
stars is similar to that of the Sun, only
much more rapid. Being bigger and
hotter than the Sun they at first burn
white or blue-white in colour, like
Rigel in the constellation Orion,
about 850 light years away and
50 000 times more luminous than
the Sun. As such stars run out of
hydrogen at the centre and start to
expand, they become red supergiants like Betelgeuse, mentioned
earlier, or Antares in Scorpius, 430
light years away and with an estimated diameter of 285 times that of

the Sun. At this point, their evolution becomes different from that of
less massive stars. Whereas stars like
the Sun stop at the helium-burning
stage, red supergiant stars continue
to get hotter and hotter at the core so
that a whole range of complex
nuclear reactions can take place.

After the fusion of helium at a
star's centre, a core of carbon is left.
The greater gravity of massive stars
– those, say, ten times heavier than
the Sun or more – squeezes this core
until it reaches the critical temperature of 600 million °C, at which
carbon fuses to form magnesium,
releasing intense heat. Next, as the
centre of the star gets even hotter,
the magnesium enters into reactions
to produce other substances; these
substances enter into more reactions,
and so on. The processes of burning,
squeezing, and more burning continue at a runaway rate, building up
a mixture of elements at and around
the star's core. Outwardly, the supergiant burns bigger and brighter than
ever.

Inwardly, though, the star is head-
ing for an energy crisis. The day of
reckoning comes once its central
temperature reaches 3 500 million

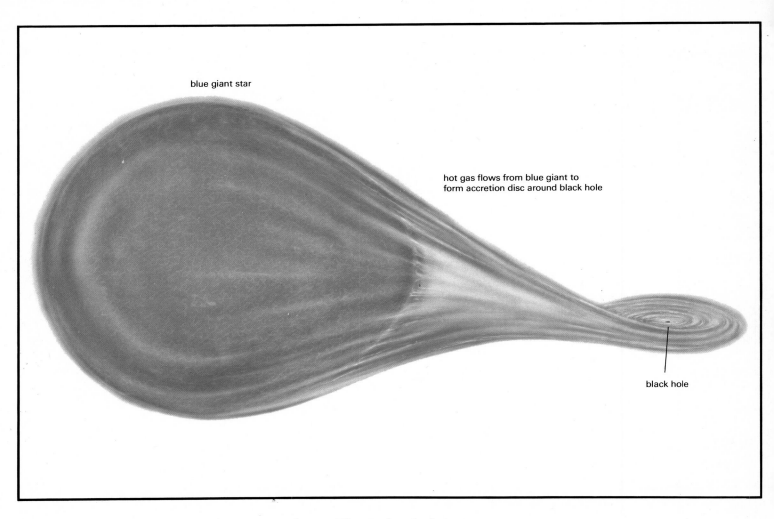

blue giant star

hot gas flows from blue giant to
form accretion disc around black hole

black hole

°C, at which iron nuclei are being
formed. Because of the nature of its
atomic structure, the fusion of iron
does not release heat, but consumes
it. With its internal power supply
switched off, the stricken star quickly
collapses in upon itself. As the outer
layers of the star cascade down upon
the core, they ignite in one final
explosion. The star has become one
of the most violent phenomena in
nature – a supernova.

In the nuclear holocaust of a supernova, all the chemical elements in
nature are synthesized and scattered
into space, where they mix with the
existing hydrogen and helium in
nebulae, ready to be collected up
into new stars and, possibly, planets.
The atoms of our planet Earth and
of our bodies were formed and
scattered into space by ancient supernovae.

The Crab nebula in Taurus is the
shattered remains of a star which was
seen by Oriental astronomers to
explode in AD 1054. Although the
Crab supernova was visible for over
21 months, and at its brightest could
be seen in daylight, no western
records of it exist, perhaps because
European astronomers were then
still shackled by the Greek doctrine
that the heavens were perfect and
unchanging, and thus preferred to
ignore this embarrassing celestial

outburst. The Crab nebula is a strong
source of radio waves, as are the
remnants of other supernovae. The
last two supernovae seen in our
Galaxy were recorded by Tycho
Brahe and Johannes Kepler in 1572
and 1604 respectively. A supernova
is estimated to occur about every 50
years in galaxies like ours, so we are
long overdue for another one. Until
then, astronomers are restricted to
observing supernovae in other
galaxies.

A supernova brightens over a few
days by thousands of millions of
times, far more than an ordinary
nova. At its brightest, a supernova
can rival the combined output of
all the stars in a galaxy. Half the star's
original mass, or more, may be
thrown off at speeds of up to 10 000
kilometres per second (6 000 miles
per second). The wisps of gas dis-
perse into space, like the Veil nebula
in Cygnus, eventually disappearing
from sight after perhaps 100 000
years.

What happens to the core of the
star left behind after a supernova
explosion? Without the internal
energy source of its nuclear fires to
sustain it, the core collapses to form
a tiny, compressed star even smaller
and denser than a white dwarf. The
strong inward pull of the heavy
core's gravity, aided by the tremen-

Above
Artist's impression of Cygnus X-1, an
X-ray source in the constellation Cygnus,
that is believed to contain a black hole.
The visible star, catalogued as HDE
226868, is a blue giant star. Hot gas flows
from its surface to form a spinning disc
around a nearby black hole. As the gas
plummets into the black hole it heats up
to temperatures of millions of degrees
Centigrade, emitting X-rays which are
detected by satellites orbiting the Earth.

Above right
Stars several times the mass of the Sun
explode as supernovae at the ends of their
lives, like the Crab nebula in Taurus,
which is the remains of a star seen by
Oriental astronomers to flare up in
AD 1054.

Right
Pulsars are tiny, super-dense stars, left
behind after supernova explosions, that
give off flashes of radiation as they spin.
This is the pulsar at the centre of the Crab
nebula, which flashes on and off thirty
times a second.

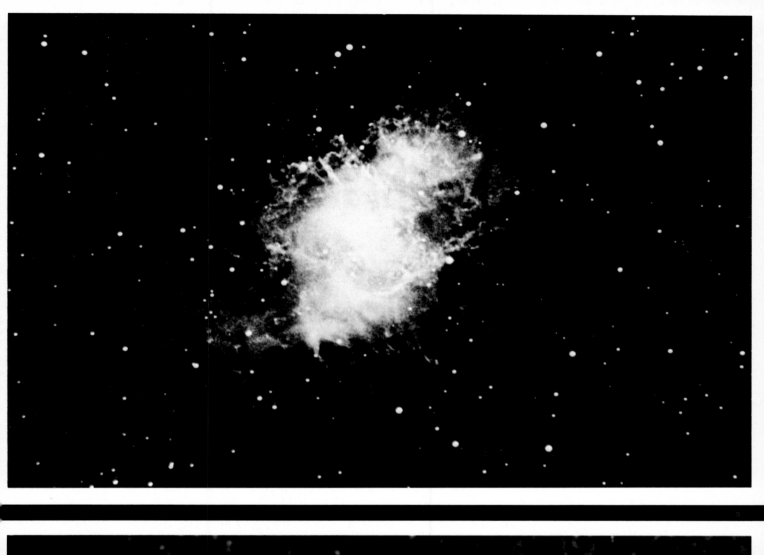
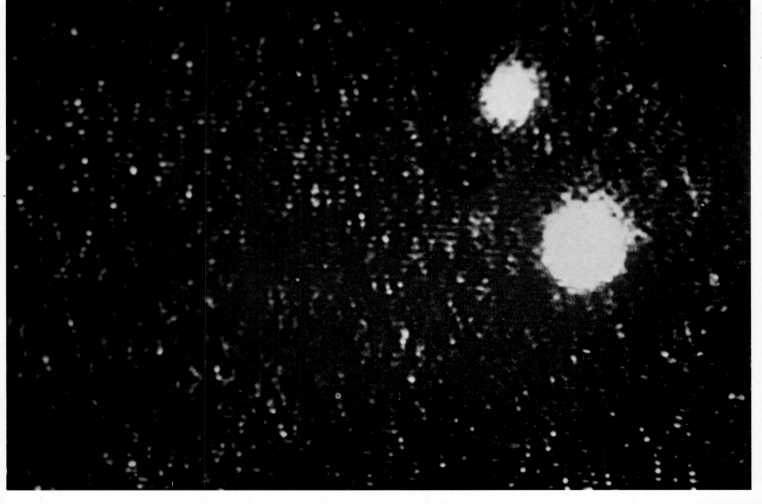

dous pressures of the supernova explosion in the layers above it, crush the electrons and protons of the core's atoms together to form the electrically neutral particles called neutrons. The resulting object is therefore termed a neutron star.

Whereas a white dwarf contains as much matter as the Sun crammed into a ball the size of the Earth, a neutron star has the mass of perhaps two Suns squashed into a sphere no more than 20 kilometres (12 miles) across. The density is such that a thimbleful of neutron star material would weigh 1 000 million tonnes.

Neutron stars were predicted by theorists as long ago as 1939, but at the time there seemed little chance of detecting them. Then, in 1967, radio astronomers at Cambridge, England, discovered the mysteriously pulsing radio sources which became known as pulsars. It soon became clear that these were tiny rapidly rotating stars that sent out a shaft of energy like a lighthouse beam each time they turned, and the only stars small enough to spin that quickly were neutron stars. How do pulsars pulse? According to the most popular view, the neutron star's strong magnetic field prevents radiation from escaping except at the magnetic poles. Therefore, each time the star's magnetic pole sweeps across our line of sight we see a flash. Pulsars slow down with age, and eventually fade away.

Approximately 150 pulsars are now known, with periods ranging from thirty pulses a second to once nearly every 4 seconds. The fastest-flashing pulsar lies at the heart of the Crab nebula; it is the compressed core of the star that was seen to explode in 1054, and underlines the fact that pulsars and neutron stars are really the same thing. This star is bright enough to show up on photographs, and had long been suspected as the supernova remnant. Once astronomers knew what to look for, in 1968, they found that this star was flashing optically thirty times a second, the same rate as the radio pulses. Only one other pulsar, in the southern constellation Vela, has been detected optically; it is the faintest star ever identified, over ten million times too dim to be seen with the naked eye.

Neutron stars are believed to exist in many of the X-ray sources detected by satellites in recent years. These sources are double-star systems in which one star of the pair has evidently already ended its life in a supernova. Gas from the ordinary star plunges into the strong gravitational field of the tiny neutron star, heating up to temperatures of millions of degrees and emitting X-rays.

One X-ray source, known as Cygnus X-1, contains evidence of an object even more remarkable than a neutron star. The visible companion star of Cygnus X-1 has been identified as a blue supergiant star which bears the catalogue number HDE 226868. Observations of this star show that the invisible X-ray source which orbits it has a mass of at least 8 Suns. According to theory, if the core left behind by a supernova weighs more than about 3 solar masses, then its own gravitational pull will compress it even beyond the stage of a neutron star. (Note that we are here talking about the remains of dead stars. While a star is still burning the release of energy from inside prevents it collapsing.) There is no known force that can hold up a dead star weighing more than 3 Suns against its own gravity. It gets smaller and smaller, denser and denser, until eventually it vanishes from sight. It has become a *black hole*.

At the centre of a black hole, the original star has been compressed to an infinitely small point, of infinitely high density; in effect, the matter of which the former star was made has been crushed out of existence. Around this central point is a gravitational boundary known as the event horizon from within which nothing can escape, not even light. Thus a black hole is completely invisible. In the case of a 3-solar-mass black hole, the event horizon has a diameter of about 18 kilometres (11 miles), but is larger for greater masses.

Although nothing can get out of a black hole, matter can fall in. Imagine the case of a double star system in which one star has already burned out and formed a black hole, rather than a neutron star. Gas will flow from the companion star towards the black hole, heating up and emitting X-rays, as in the case of gas falling on to a neutron star. Although the black hole cannot be seen directly, the X-ray emission gives it away. This is believed to be what is happening in the case of Cygnus X-1.

According to one estimate, there could be as many as 10 million black holes in our galaxy, formed by the supernova explosions of massive stars. Astronomers are continuing to hunt for more examples of these objects, which are among the most bizarre products of the universe.

Formation of neutron stars and black holes. A giant star explodes as a supernova, throwing off its outer layers, and the star's core left behind is compressed by the force of the explosion. It may become a tiny neutron star, smaller than the Earth, or it may continue to collapse until its gravity gets so strong that light cannot escape. It disappears from the universe as if down a bottomless well.

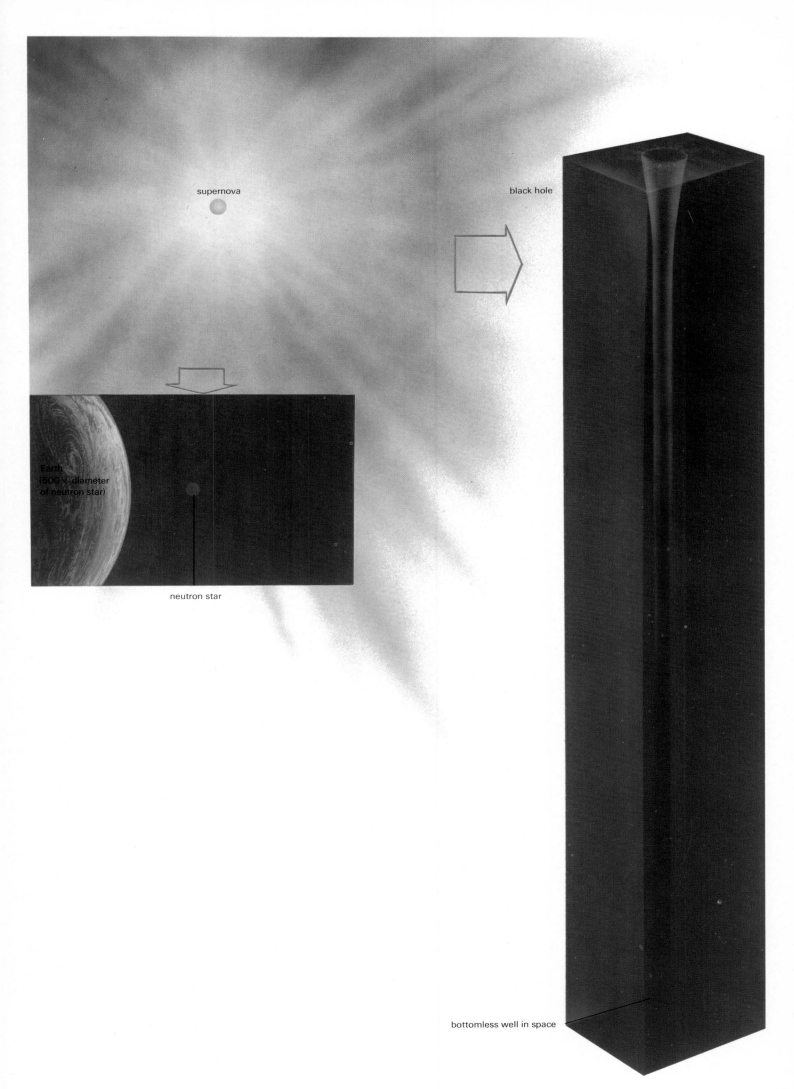

supernova

black hole

Earth
(500 × diameter
of neutron star)

neutron star

bottomless well in space

73

Galaxies
and the universe

plan view

approximate position of Sun in the galaxy

globular clusters

side view

No-one knows how vast the universe is. Our concept of the universe has grown from the cosy, Earth-centred model of the Greeks to the dizzying vision of today in which the Earth orbits an ordinary star in the outer regions of a galaxy of a myriad other stars, which is itself only one of countless other galaxies in a universe of expanding space that may go on without end. The largest telescopes are probing the remotest regions of the universe in search of further clues to its possible origin.

Until early this century, astronomers still accepted the view of Sir William Herschel in 1784 that the Sun lay near the centre of a lens-shaped collection of stars, the galaxy, about five times as long as it was thick, that was presumed to mark the extent of the entire universe. Then, in 1917, the American astronomer Harlow Shapley showed that the galaxy was twice as large as previously supposed, and that the Sun was nowhere near the centre. What Shapley did was to measure the distances to globular clusters of stars which are scattered in a halo around our galaxy. Globular clusters are ball-shaped aggregations of 100 000 or more old stars formed early in the history of our galaxy, and they include the 'heartbeat' type of variable stars described in the previous chapter. Shapley used these stars to measure the distances to the clusters, which therefore gave him an idea of the overall size of the galaxy. He noted that the Sun did not lie symmetrically at the centre of the halo of globular clusters, but instead was shifted to one side. This meant that the Sun could not be centrally placed in the galaxy. Shapley's results, as refined by later work, showed that the galaxy is 100 000 light years in diameter, and that the Sun lies 30 000 light years from the centre. This was the first accurate measurement of the size of our galaxy and the Sun's position in it, but it still left open the question of what, if anything, lay beyond our galaxy.

William Herschel in the late eighteenth century had also addressed himself to this problem when he studied the fuzzy patches known as nebulae which puzzled astronomers: were these part of the galaxy, or beyond it? With Herschel's 122-centimetre (48-inch) reflector, then the largest in the world, some nebulae could be resolved into nearby clusters of stars, but others remained obstinately hazy. Certain of these, such as the famous nebula in Orion, were undoubtedly glowing clouds of gas within the galaxy, but they were the minority. In Ireland, Lord Rosse (1800–1867) built an even larger telescope than Herschel's to continue study of nebulae. With this 183-centimetre (72-inch) reflector, completed in 1845, Rosse found that certain nebulae had a spiral structure, notably the object in the constella-

Left
With his giant telescope, Lord Rosse examined nebulae and star clusters. This is his drawing of the whirlpool galaxy, M 51, in Canes Venatici, the spiral shape of which Rosse resolved for the first time.

Below
The Andromeda galaxy, M 31, is a famous spiral galaxy, 2·2 million light years away. Our own galaxy would look similar to this when seen from outside.

Right
Lord Rosse's 183-centimetre (72-inch) reflecting telescope at Birr Castle, Parsonstown, Ireland, was the largest in the world when opened in 1845. It was mounted between two high walls, which severely limited its mobility and view of the sky.

tion Canes Venatici known as M51 (its number in the catalogue of nebulae compiled by the French astronomer Charles Messier (1730–1817)). But the significance of his observations did not become clear until 75 years later when the American astronomer Edwin Hubble used the newly opened Mount Wilson 2·5-metre (100-inch) reflector for a closer look at the spiral nebulae.

In 1924, Hubble photographed faint stars in the outer regions of the so-called Andromeda nebula, a well-known spiral, which showed that it was actually a separate star system, or galaxy, similar to our own. By implication, therefore, *all* the thousands of spiral nebulae then known to astronomers were actually separate galaxies. This discovery opened up the vision of an awesomely vast universe with galaxies scattered like islands in a sea of space. Today it is estimated that there are thousands of millions of galaxies visible with the largest telescopes. On a clear night, the Andromeda galaxy, numbered

M31 in the Messier catalogue, can be seen as a faint hazy patch even without binoculars; it is the farthest that the naked eye can see. According to modern figures, the Andromeda galaxy is 2·2 million light years away, so we see it as it was when our ape-ancestors roamed the plains of Africa. Yet it is still one of our closest galactic neighbours.

Hubble went on to examine many other galaxies, and in 1925 produced a classification scheme that is still used today. In Hubble's classification, over half of all galaxies are normal Catherine-wheel shaped spirals, like M31 and our own galaxy. These have a bulging heart of old stars, from which curving arms of younger stars radiate. About a quarter of all galaxies are termed barred spirals, because the spiral arms curve from the ends of a straight bar of stars that runs across the galaxy's centre. Apart from a few per cent of irregular galaxies which have no obvious shape at all, most other galaxies are classified as ellipticals. These have no

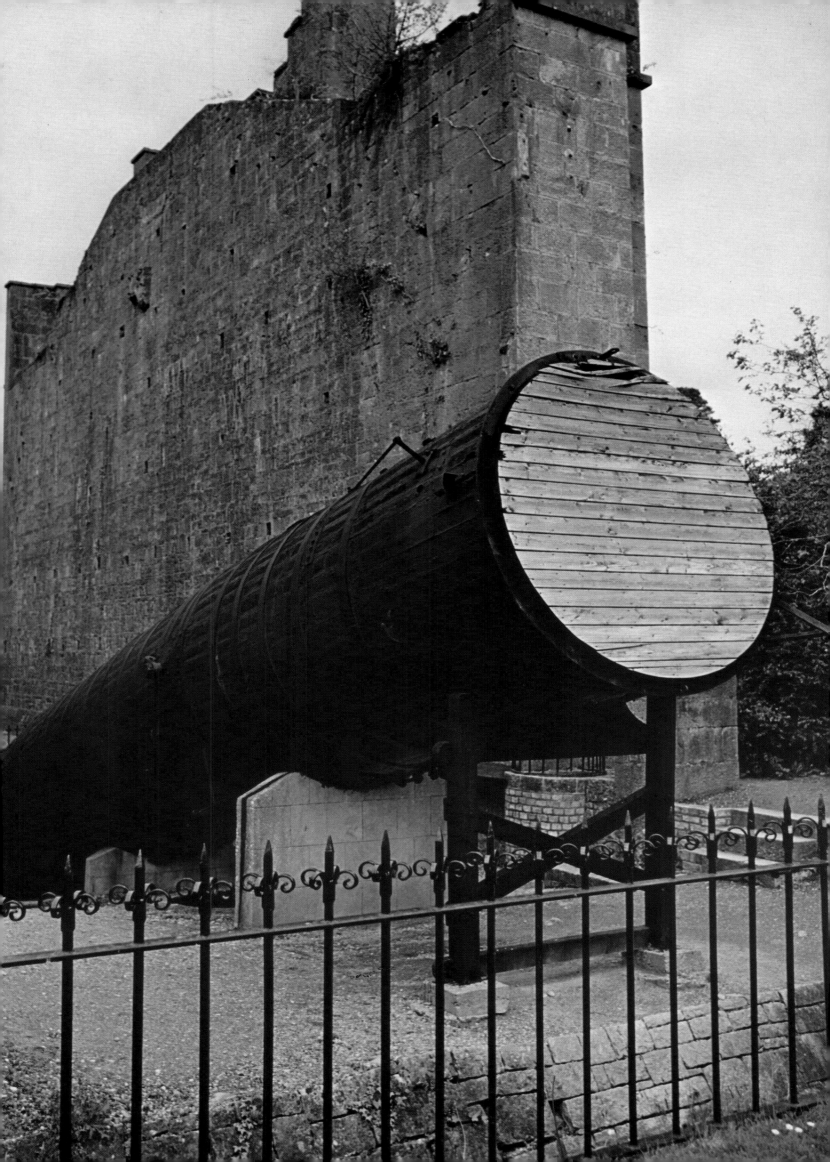

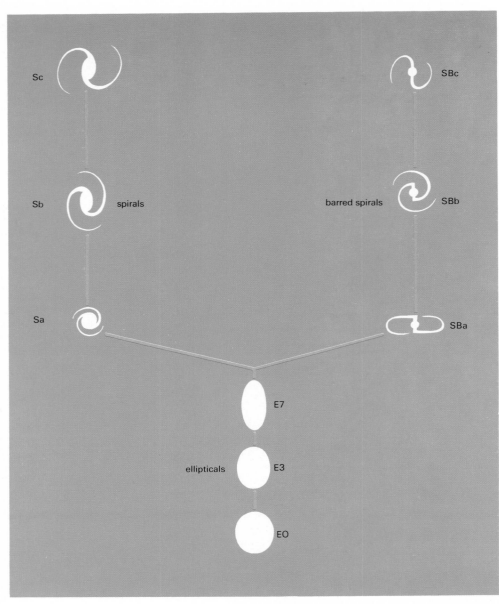

Sc

Sb   spirals

Sa

SBc

barred spirals   SBb

SBa

E7

ellipticals   E3

E0

Left
Edwin Hubble, the American astronomer, classified galaxies according to whether they were spirals, barred spirals, or elliptical in shape.

Below
Spiral galaxy NGC 253 in the constellation Sculptor.

Right
The Magellanic Clouds are satellite galaxies of our own. This is the larger Magellanic cloud, photographed in ultra-violet light from the surface of the Moon by the astronauts of Apollo 16. The areas containing the hottest stars are colour-coded to appear red, yellow, or orange, while the dark sky background appears blue.

Below right
Spiral galaxy M 51, the whirlpool; compare with Lord Rosse's drawing of the same object on page 78. A satellite galaxy appears to be attached to the end of one of the spiral arms.

arms, but are simply a crowded mass of stars ranging from near-spherical to a cross-sectional shape like that of a rugby ball. Elliptical galaxies have a wide range of sizes, from faint dwarf ellipticals, only 5 000 light years or so in diameter and containing no more than a million stars, to supergiant ellipticals, the brightest known galaxies in the universe, which can contain ten million million stars in a diameter of several million light years. Spiral galaxies, by contrast, are more constant in size: they have between 1 000 million to a million million stars, and their diameters range from 20 000 to several hundred thousand light years.

The spiral structure of our galaxy has been traced in detail by radio astronomers, who pick up radiation of 21-centimetre wavelength from the hydrogen gas that lies plentifully between the stars in the galaxy's curving arms. It is from this gas that new stars continually form. Our galaxy is estimated to contain 100 000 million stars, making it one of the largest spirals. The faint band of

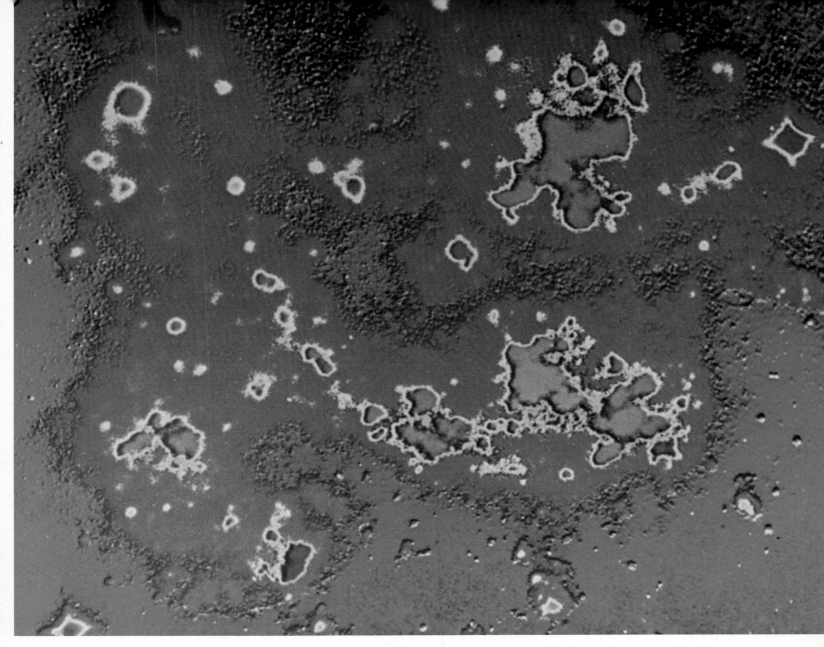

stars that crosses the sky, the Milky Way, is the rest of our galaxy as seen from inside; the name Milky Way is often used as a synonym for our galaxy. All the stars are moving as the galaxy rotates. Our Sun takes about 225 million years to orbit the galaxy, so that it has gone round only about twenty times since it was born. The stars' movements, known as *proper motions*, are too slight to be visible to the naked eye, but over many thousands of years they will gradually change the shapes of the constellations.

Two irregular-shaped satellite galaxies known as the Magellanic Clouds accompany our Milky Way. Named for the round-the-world explorer Ferdinand Magellan, they are visible as faintly luminous clouds in the southern hemisphere. The larger of the two lies about 160 000 light years away and contains approximately 5 000 million stars, about one-twentieth the mass of our galaxy. The smaller Magellanic Cloud, with about 2 000 million stars, lies slightly farther away, 200 000 light years.

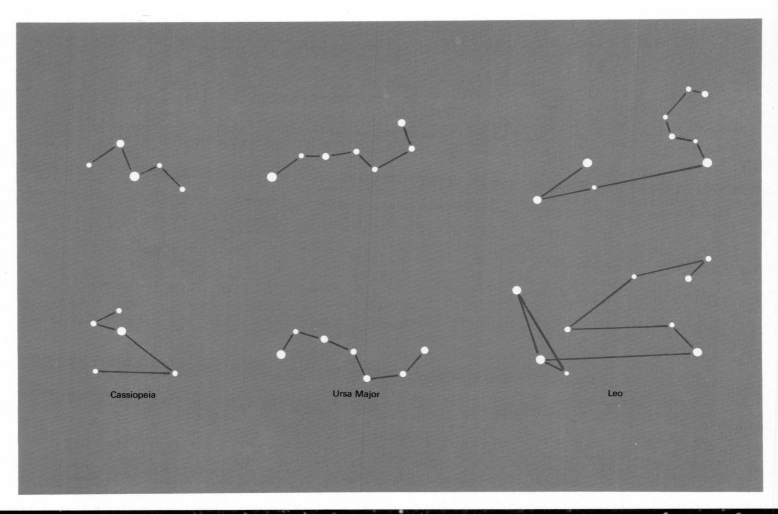

Cassiopeia   Ursa Major   Leo

Left
Movements of stars in their orbits around the galaxy cause constellations to change in shape. Here, three familiar constellations are shown as they appear today, with their predicted appearance 100 000 years hence.

Below left
Spiral galaxy M 33 in Triangulum is approximately 2 million light years away. It is the third largest member of the local group of galaxies, being smaller than our galaxy and M 31.

Below
Our galaxy is one of a group of about twenty other known galaxies called the local group.

The Clouds are 24 000 and 12 000 light years in diameter, respectively.

The Magellanic Clouds are our closest neighbours in a cluster of about twenty galaxies known as the local group. Most galaxies throughout the universe seem to cluster in groups, some containing up to several thousand members. In our local group the largest member is the Andromeda spiral, M31, which contains about twice as many stars as the Milky Way and is about 50 per cent greater in diameter. Two satellite galaxies, similar to the Magellanic Clouds, accompany M31, along with several smaller and fainter companions, recently discovered. A spiral galaxy known as M33 in the constel-

lation Triangulum is the third major member of the local group, although it is only about half the diameter of our galaxy and contains perhaps one-tenth the number of stars. It is over 2 million light years away, the same distance as the Andromeda galaxy. All the remaining members of the local group are dwarf elliptical or irregular galaxies.

Our local group is bound together by its own gravitation. As Edwin Hubble looked deeper into space with the Mount Wilson telescope, he found that other galaxies appeared to be moving away from us at speeds that increased with their distance. The galaxies' movements could be told from the so-called *red shift* of

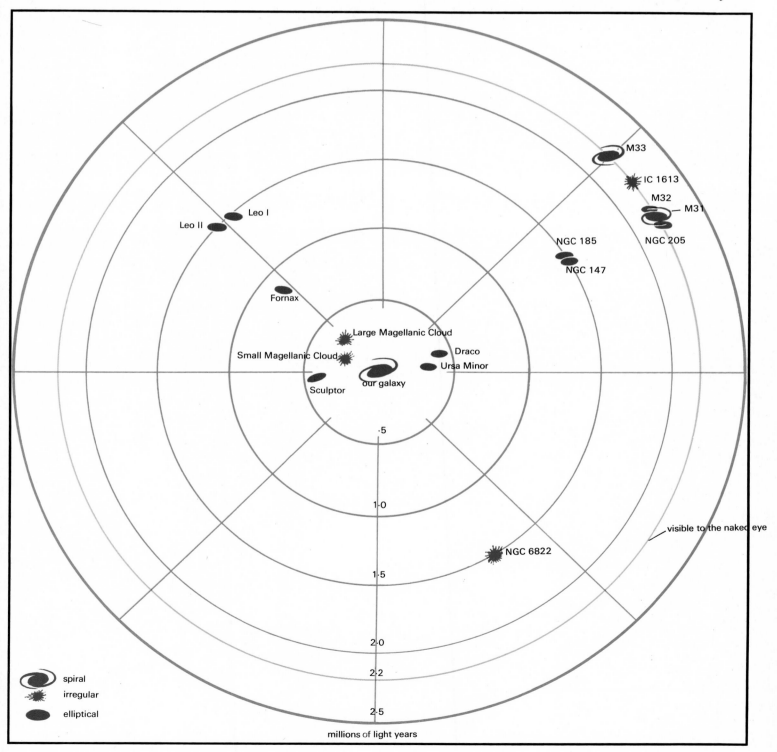

spiral

irregular

elliptical

millions of light years

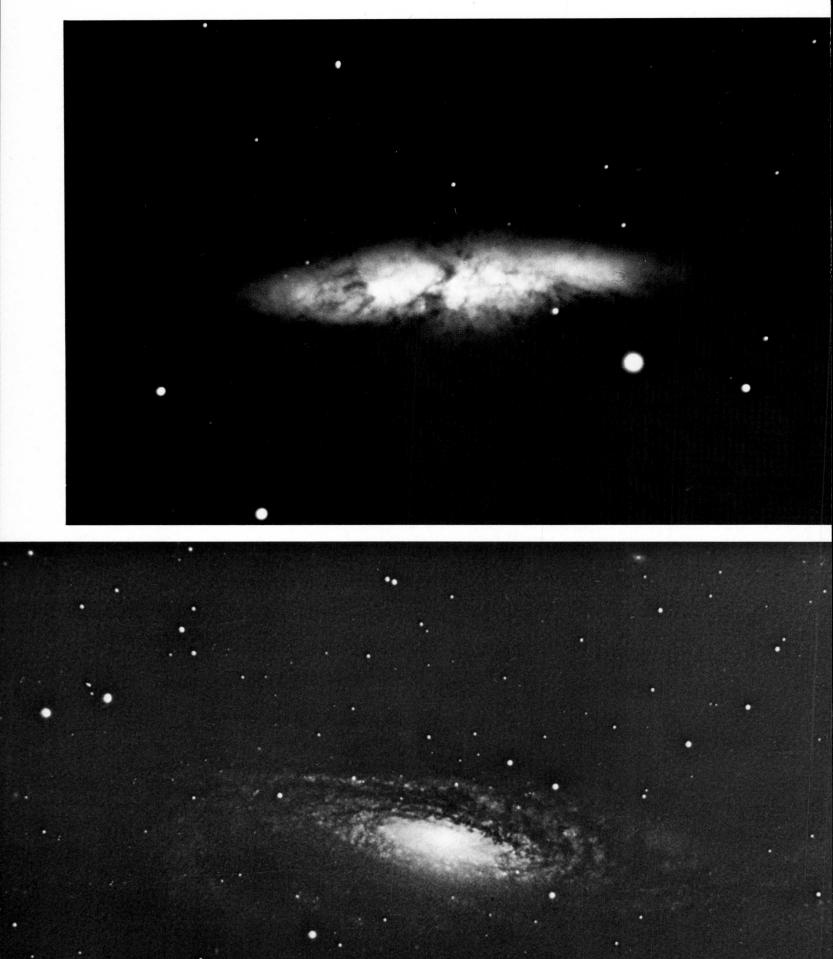

Above left
M 82 in the constellation Ursa Major is a peculiar galaxy that gives out copious radio waves. It is believed to be the site of an enormous explosion.

Left
Spiral galaxy NGC 7331 in Pegasus.

Above
The expanding universe. Galaxies are receding from us in all directions, the speed of recession being proportional to the distances of the galaxies.

their light, a lengthening of wavelengths caused by recession; since red wavelengths are longer than blue ones, a lengthening of wavelength means a reddening of light, hence the term red shift. Another name for this change of wavelength is the Doppler effect, after the German physicist Christian Doppler (1803–1853), and it is also used to detect the motions of stars. The red shift of light from the galaxies told that they were receding; and, as Hubble painstakingly measured the distances to the galaxies, he found that the farthest ones were receding the fastest. In other words, the universe as a whole seemed to be expanding. Hubble's sensational discovery of the expansion of the universe, announced in 1929, is a keystone of modern cosmology, the branch of astronomy

concerned with the origin and evolution of the universe.

This does not mean, though, that our galaxy is the centre of the universe. As the universe expands, each galaxy moves away from the others because the space between them has grown. An observer on any one galaxy will see exactly the same effect as an observer on any other galaxy. Therefore, there is no 'centre' to the universe. First Shapley, by dethroning the Sun from the centre of the galaxy, and then Hubble, with his demonstration that the galaxy is as helpless as an unmoored ship against the tide of the universe, had wrought a revolution even more astounding than that in which Galileo and Kepler affirmed the theory of Copernicus, approximately 300 years earlier.

Big Bang

universe expands and thins out

Knowledge that the universe is expanding led the Belgian astronomer Georges Lemaitre (1894–1966) to suggest that the universe began in a giant explosion, now known as the Big Bang; the galaxies are pieces from that explosion flying outwards. Modern measurements of the expansion of the universe show that the galaxies are receding at a rate of about 16 kilometres (10 miles) per second for every million light years of distance; this figure is known as *Hubble's constant* and is important because it relates a galaxy's distance to its speed of movement. Once the red shift in a galaxy's light has been measured, therefore, astronomers can deduce its distance by reference to Hubble's constant. Hubble's constant also reveals the age of the universe, because by tracking back the rate of expansion astronomers can deduce when the Big Bang explosion must have taken place. Current estimates suggest that 20 000 million years has elapsed since the Big Bang.

In 1948, three astronomers working in Britain, Thomas Gold (b. 1920), Hermann Bondi (b. 1919), and Fred Hoyle (b. 1915) put forward a very different theory of the universe. They proposed that the universe did not have a beginning, but has always existed. Instead of there being a single instant of creation, new matter continually comes into being to fill the space left as the universe expands, so that if we could see the universe at any time in the past or the future it would look much the same as it does today. This controversial theory is called the Steady State theory.

However, observations have indicated that the universe was not the same in the past. Although it seems impossible to turn back the clock to see what the universe looked like in the past, this is exactly what astronomers can do by looking far off into space. Because light takes a finite time to reach us, we see objects in the universe not as they appear now but as they were when the light left them.

Left
According to modern views, our universe began in a giant explosion called the Big Bang, from which it has been expanding ever since. In the Big Bang theory, as the universe expands the galaxies in it thin out.

Right
An alternative theory to the Big Bang is the Steady State theory, according to which the universe has always existed, material being continually created to fill space as the universe expands.

new material is created as universe expands

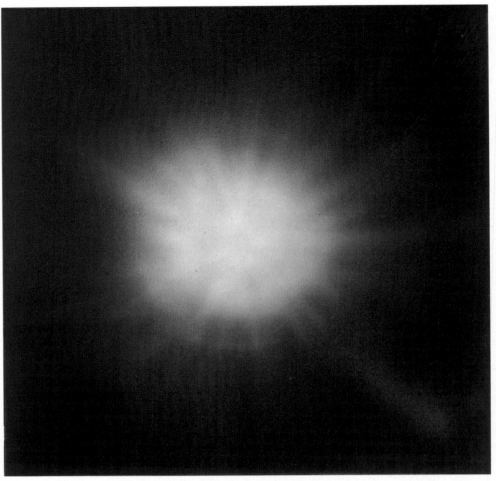

Below
Many galaxies and quasars emit strong radio waves. This is the giant elliptical galaxy called NGC 5128 in the constellation Centaurus, as seen through an optical telescope. In radio telescopes, however, it is found to be surrounded by vast areas of invisible gas that emit radio waves. The radio-emitting areas appear to have been ejected in explosions from the central galaxy, which is also known as Centaurus A.

For instance, we see the Sun as it was 8·3 minutes ago, Sirius as it was 8·7 years ago, and the Andromeda galaxy as it was 2·2 million years ago. Telescopes are time machines; they allow astronomers to see the most remote areas of the universe as they appeared thousands of millions of years ago. The farthest known galaxy, identified in 1975, is a supergiant elliptical called 3C 123 which is receding at 45 per cent the speed of light, which places it at a distance of over 8 000 million light years; there-fore we see it as it appeared long before the Earth was born. Beyond this, galaxies are too faint to be seen optically, but they can still be detected by radio astronomers. During the 1950s radio astronomers began counting the numbers of radio sources deep in the universe. They found that the weakest sources, which were presumably the most remote, were more numerous than expected on the Steady State theory. It seemed as though the universe looked differ-ent in the past, which would mean it was evolving, as the Big Bang theory required.

Bigger trouble for the Steady State theory came as astronomers began to identify certain of the radio sources optically. Some of them were clearly associated with known gal-axies, albeit peculiar-looking ones, but others were centred on what looked like distant blue stars. In 1963, the American astronomer Maarten Schmidt (b. 1929), examining the light from one of these objects, known as 3C 273 (its number in the

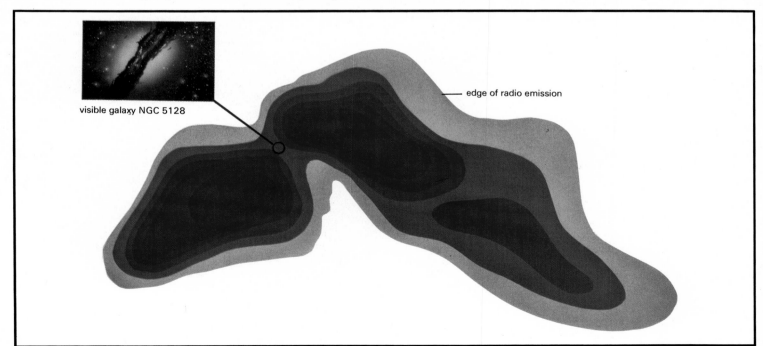

visible galaxy NGC 5128

edge of radio emission

third catalogue of radio sources compiled at Cambridge, England), found that it had a red shift so great that it must be far off in the universe, and was therefore not a star at all. The red shift of 3C 273 was 16 per cent the speed of light, meaning that it was moving at 48 000 kilometres (30 000 miles) per second; from the Hubble constant, it must be 3 000 million light years away. At the time, this was an unprecedented distance, but soon other star-like objects with even greater red shifts were identified. They became known as quasi-stellar objects, shortened to *quasars*.

Quasars have proved to be the most astounding objects in the universe. Less than one light year in diameter, they nevertheless pack as much energy as thousands of galaxies combined, so that they are

visible over vast distances at which normal galaxies cannot be seen. Quasar OQ 172 was discovered, in 1973, to be receding at 91 per cent the speed of light, which means that it lies 17 000 million light years away; it is the farthest known object in the universe. Quasars present astronomers with an energy crisis, because no one is certain how so much luminosity can be produced in such a relatively tiny space. One early attempt to avoid this problem was the suggestion that quasars are not far off at all, but are instead much smaller and fainter objects that have been ejected at high speed from our galaxy. However, observations of quasars have not revealed the signs of motion that would be expected if they were really nearby, and neither are there any similar objects being

M 101, a famous spiral galaxy 23·5 million light years away in the constellation Ursa Major.

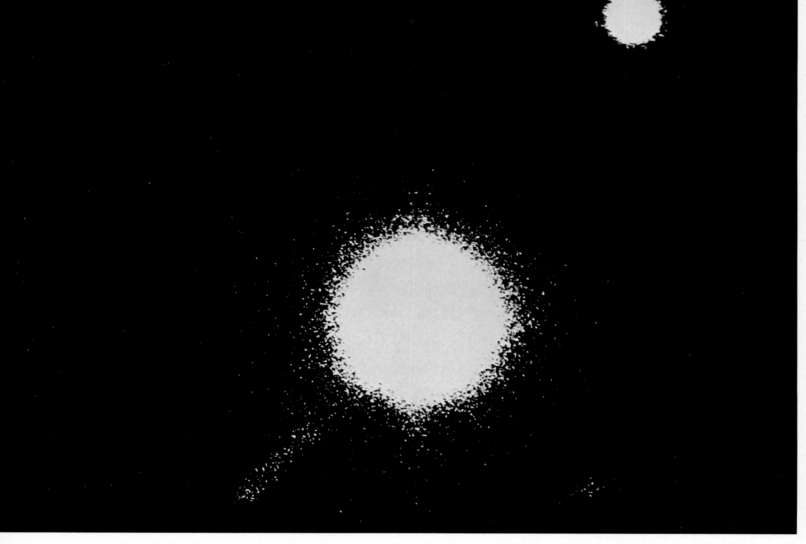

Quasar 3C 273 was the first to have its red shift measured. It is 3 000 million light years away. Quasars get their name because they look star-like in photographs, but this quasar appears to be ejecting a jet of gas. Both the centre of the quasar and the jet are sources of radio waves.

ejected from other galaxies. Some astronomers have now begun to wonder in desperation whether the red shift of quasars is produced by their motion at all, or whether it has some other cause which would therefore mean that they are not so distant or luminous as otherwise assumed. However, it is generally accepted that quasars are in fact the most distant objects in the universe and that, since no such objects are observed nearby, the universe must have looked very different in the past, in contradiction of the Steady State theory.

To confuse matters further, not all quasars emit radio waves. Those that do, have radio emissions from two optically invisible clouds, one on either side of the visible quasar. This double structure is the same as that shown by radio galaxies, which are visible galaxies that emit strong amounts of radio waves. One famous example is the strange-looking galaxy known as NGC 5128, its number in the *New General Catalogue of Nebulae and Clusters* published in 1888 by the Danish astronomer J. L. E. Dreyer (1852–1926). This object looks like a supergiant elliptical galaxy ringed by a band of dark dust. Radio-emitting regions flank it, as though ejected in one or more

giant explosions in the past. Another radio galaxy, 3C 276, is the largest known object in the universe, stretching for over 20 million light years from the tip of one radio-emitting cloud to the other, ten times the distance from ourselves to the Andromeda galaxy.

Radio galaxies do not give out as much energy as quasars, but perhaps that is because they have quietened down with age. Another clue to the nature of quasars comes from spiral galaxies with brilliant nuclei, known as Seyfert galaxies after their discoverer Carl Seyfert (1911–1960), an American astronomer. These seem to be a midway stage between quasars and normal galaxies. If Seyfert galaxies were moved farther away, only their brilliant centres would be visible, and they would look like quasars. In fact, some quasars have been found to be surrounded by a fuzz, like the faint outer regions of a galaxy. Therefore, most astronomers now believe that quasars are the extremely active centres of galaxies at an early stage in their evolution.

A coherent picture is at last beginning to emerge from all this. If theories of stellar evolution described in the previous chapter are correct, giant black holes would be expected to form at the centres of galaxies from the death of massive stars. These black holes would grow by the influx of material to a mass of a million Suns or so, at which stage gravity would tear apart nearby stars and then suck in the gas. Such a massive black hole swallowing matter at the heart of a galaxy could be the energy source that powers quasars, and ejects radio-emitting clouds. When the quasar switches off optically, perhaps because it has exhausted all the available material at the galaxy's heart, the radio emission will live on around it as a fossil relic. Such an object is what we call a radio galaxy. Eventually, the radio emission will fade away, leaving a normal-looking galaxy. However, it must be said that this scenario is highly speculative, and not all astronomers support it. It is not even clear, for instance, whether all galaxies go through a quasar stage in their evolution, or whether it is confined to certain types of massive galaxy, such as the supergiant ellipticals. Our galaxy and the other members of the local group presumably never went through a quasar stage.

Astronomers, in thinking along these lines, have tacitly accepted the Big Bang theory. However, the major body blow to the Steady State ideas came not from quasars but from the observation by radio astronomers in 1965 that the universe seems to be filled with a slight background warmth. The universe, in fact, is not totally cold, but has a temperature of $2.7°C$ above absolute zero (absolute zero is the lowest temperature possible, equivalent to $-273°C$). This cosmic background radiation is interpreted as being heat left over from the Big Bang, and its existence had actually been predicted as long ago as 1948 by the American astronomer George Gamow (1904–1968), a major supporter of the Big Bang theory. With its discovery, all remaining support for the Steady State theory dwindled.

An intriguing variant on the Big Bang theory suggests that the universe is continually blowing up and collapsing again in cycles; this was termed the oscillating universe. An oscillating universe would also have no beginning or end, although it might be very different in each cycle. If we could return thousands of millions of years hence, according to this theory, we might be in a contracting universe, in which the galaxies were falling back together towards the next Big Bang.

How can we tell if the universe is oscillating? Imagine a stone thrown upwards. As we watch it, it slows down, and falls back again. But if we managed to throw it fast enough, it would keep on going and never return. Similarly, if the galaxies are moving away fast enough they will never return. Astronomers examining the red shifts of the farthest galaxies can find very little evidence that they are slowing down. In other words, the energy of the Big Bang threw the universe apart with such force that its own gravity will never again be able to pull it together. We live, therefore, in a continuously expanding universe, not an oscillating one.

Cosmologists now sketch the following life story of the universe and of galaxies. Twenty thousand million years ago, all the matter of the universe was compressed in a superdense state, from which it exploded in the Big Bang. According to theorists, such as the British mathematician Stephen Hawking, conditions in the Big Bang would have been so extreme that mini black holes would have formed, with the mass of a mountain (say, 1 000 million tonnes) crammed into a space about 10 million millionths of a centimetre across, roughly the size of an atomic particle. Hawking has shown that such mini black holes evaporate explosively after a given time that depends on their mass; some should be exploding today, giving out bursts of high-energy γ-rays. Since such mini black holes cannot be formed in the conditions of the

Photographic representation of the radio emission from 3C 236 as observed by the Westerbork Synthesis Radio Telescope.

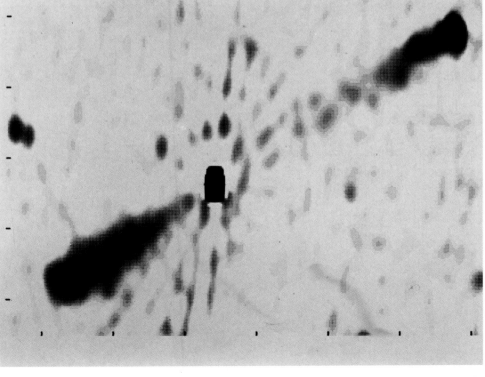

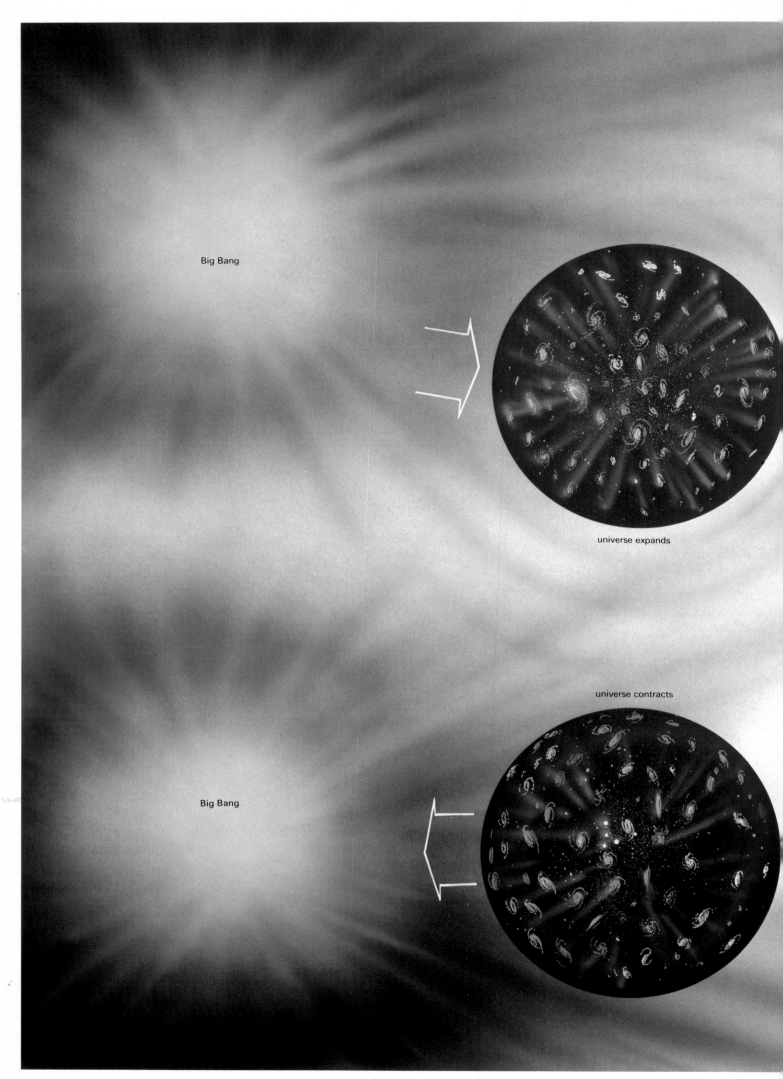

Big Bang

universe expands

universe contracts

Big Bang

A third theory of the universe says that it alternately expands and contracts in cycles. According to this theory, called the oscillating universe, the present expansion of the universe will eventually slow down and stop, to be replaced by a contraction to another Big Bang.

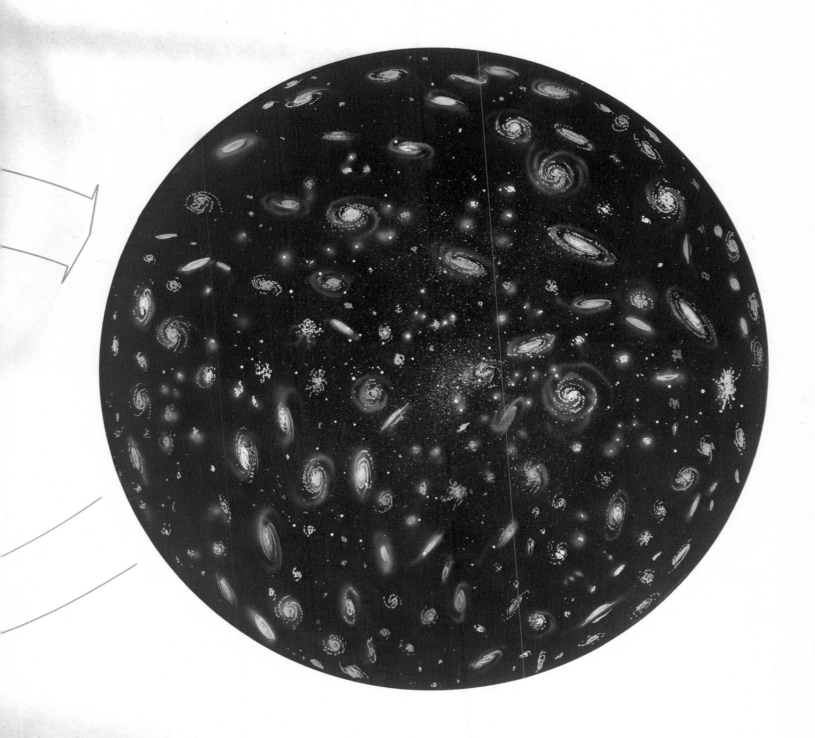

Seyfert galaxy NGC 4151. Seyfert galaxies are spiral galaxies with particularly bright nuclei; they are believed to be close relatives of quasars.

universe today, if astronomers could find γ-rays from exploding mini black holes in space this would be further powerful evidence that the universe once went through a Big-Bang-like state.

Hydrogen and helium gas flung out from the Big Bang broke up over thousands of millions of years into clumps which shrank to form galaxies. When all of a gas clump collected into stars early on, an elliptical galaxy was produced. In other cases, a disc of gas was left circling the central bulge of stars, producing a spiral galaxy. Barred spirals are believed to differ from normal spirals only in that they are rotating more rapidly, so that the stars near the centre are pulled out into two main arms.

Our galaxy began to form about 14 000 million years ago, which is the age of the oldest stars in the halo of globular clusters around the galaxy. These formed first as that massive parent gas cloud shrank, while a nucleus of stars built up at the centre. Around this nucleus the remaining gas was spread out into a disc by the galaxy's rotation, pro-

ducing the spiral arms in which younger stars were born. Then, 4 600 million years ago, our Sun and its planetary system came into being in one of those spiral arms. Now, intelligent beings sit on the third planet from the Sun and ask questions about their environment in space.

We shall continue to ask questions, for it would be foolish to think that we have the final answers to such fundamental questions as the nature and origin of the universe. For instance, it seems that the remaining gas and dust in our galaxy, and others, will one day all be collected up into stars, with no more left to make new stars. Meanwhile the universe will continue to expand, so that the galaxies will thin out in space, eventually losing sight of each other. Over millions of millions of years the universe must slowly fade out and die.

But in, say, another 50 years, our ideas may be completely different. In centuries to come, our present views of cosmology may seem as naive as those of the ancient Greeks do to us.

Index

ACKNOWLEDGEMENTS

Heather Angel (Biofotos), Farnham 37; Ardea Photographics, London 52 top (K. W. Fink); Aspect Picture Library, London 8, 23 top, 36, 40–41, 57, 60, 75, 89, 90; Bord Failte – Irish Tourist Board, Dublin 79 (B. Lynch); Bruce Coleman, London title page and 47 (M. Freeman); Hale Observatories, Pasadena, California endpapers, 26 top left, 66, 67, 68, 69, 70 top, 80, 82, 84, 94; Hamlyn Group Picture Library 15 and 17 bottom (Baynton-Williams, London), 10–11 and 12 (British Museum, London), 21 (Biblioteca Marucelliani, Florence), 17 top (Cracow University, Poland), 18 (National Maritime Museum, London); Michael Holford Library, Loughton 13 (British Museum, London), 23 bottom (Science Museum, London), 52 bottom; Los Alamos Scientific Laboratory, New Mexico 53 (W. H. Regan), 61 (B. J. Rodgers); National Aeronautics – Space Administration, Washington D.C. 28 bottom, 44 top, 45; National Portrait Gallery, London 22 bottom; Photri, Alexandria, Virginia 7, 24, 34, 35, 42–43, 70 bottom; Ann Ronan Picture Library, Loughton 19, 20, 22 top, 23 top, 25, 78; Space Frontiers, Havant 31, 44 bottom, 46, 55, 64, 76, 81; Tony Stone Associates, London 8–9; R. G. Strom, Westerbork Radio Observatory, Holland 91; Z.E.F.A., London 26–27, 29, 56.